MW00777059

Journey to the Awakening

DENISE CLAIRE

SHE Wise Publications, LLC
Brandywine, MD 20613

Journey to the Awakening/ Denise Claire —1st ed.

Paperback ISBN: 979-8-9883416-2-8

Audiobook ISBN: 979-8-9883416-3-5

Hardcover ISBN: 979-8-9883416-4-2

eBook ISBN: 979-8-9883416-7-3

Published by SHE Wise Publications, LLC

SHE Wise Publications, LCC Brandywine, MD 20613

www.shewisepublications.com

Contents

Dedication

I would like to dedicate this book to the souls of previous generations who were silenced by cruelty and fear. Especially my mother, grandmother and great grandmother – who had immense strength and courage to survive the abuse of the previous generations and who lost their voices.

To those who yearned with all their hearts and souls for their children and their children's children to have a life without fear, a life where their voices could be heard and acknowledged.

May every soul who reads this book find a better understanding of the generations who came before them. Look into your past generations to find the strength to create a world where all souls do not just live in survival mode – but promote a life of love and kindness here on Earth and live as the examples of divine love that all children are meant to see!

Evolution from Darkness to Light

"A Soul's Journey"

This is all about my soul's journey to teach God's People—

How to heal and see the truth about GOD!

How to come home to GOD—

It is a journey all souls must take.

This will give others a pathway to follow and lead them back to GOD!

SHORT MEMORIES

"Please help me!" I said in a weak voice, "I cannot breathe." Why did they put me in here? We were just playing hide and seek. In the back corner of our kitchen, we had an old washing machine; the kind from the 1950s with the wringer on the side. I was very little. They coiled me up on the inside of the drum and once they put me in, I could not get out. "Please help me, I am stuck!" I began to cry, but I was having a hard time breathing. It was such a feeling of despair and fear that I would not be able to get out. I was wedged in there pretty well. Once they realized that I really was not able to get out and I was not kidding, they panicked and tried to come over to remove me. I do not remember how they eventually got me out; I just remember being stuck and helpless.

There was something about feeling alone, scared, and not able to help myself that would become an overwhelming sense of fear throughout my childhood.

My brothers loved to play hide and seek. One day two of them convinced me to hide in the closet – then held the door handle so that I could not get out. This particular closet had an attic access panel in the ceiling. We never went in the attic: there were monsters up there, and they hurt little kids. My brothers convinced me to hide in the closet and cover up with the clothes that were on the floor so even if someone opened the door, they would not see me. I complied and they closed the door. Minutes later, I heard noises outside the door. They were scary noises: scratching on the door, ghost and monster noises – over and over. I became frightened and as I tried to open the door, I realized it was stuck. I could not turn the handle or push the door open. I called out for them to come and help me. "Anyone there?" I yelled. "I am stuck. Please come let me out." They thought it was humorous and kept me locked in there, in the dark, for quite some time. They made all sorts of scary noises and said the monsters were coming for me. I was frightened to death. I began to scream, and I think they were worried that my mother would come to see what they were doing. So, they finally opened the door to let me out.

Fear of the dark is a real thing. My entire life I was afraid of the dark. I would close all closet doors before I could go to sleep. This pattern of behavior continued well into adulthood; I would even close all closet doors in my children's rooms, as they were growing up, when I tucked them in at night.

WHEN MOM WAS NOT LOOKING

Mom would go next door to have a cup of tea with the neighbor. I am not sure how long she would be gone. It only took a few minutes for the older sibling to grab one of the younger kids throw us to the floor and make everyone else hit the person on the floor. If you did not comply, you were next on the ground with everyone ganging up on you. If we tried to tell on him, the next time was even worse. We did try to tell our mom; I'm not sure if she ever believed us, as she tended to brush things off.

It always seemed that I was the outcast. From a very young age, my older siblings told me this story about how I was not really part of the family. They told me that my mother found me on the other side of the stone wall, wrapped up in a dirty blanket with a snotty, runny nose, and I was filthy. She felt sorry for me and brought me home. I was told that I was adopted, and they even had a name all made up for me and told me no one loved me, so they just left me there hungry and crying. I was always trying to be good so no one would send me away, because I had no place to go. I always felt no one wanted me from the time I was born. I truly believed that I was adopted, until I was about 12 years old when I finally got the courage to confront my mother and ask the question: was I really adopted, and had she truly found me on the other side of the wall?

ANOTHER MEMORY

I was a little girl about 5 years old. Yes, that is where the intense memories truly begin. These two recollections from my childhood that stayed with me always; nothing much resonated with me before these events. There were six children in the family. We each received one toy and one article of clothing for Christmas. There was also always a family gift, typically a game or two, for all to share. We did not have much, but to me it was everything. Looking at the neatly wrapped gifts under the lighted Christmas tree, in the middle of the picture window in the living room, always brought me great joy. That beautiful tree with its brightly colored lights was just wonderful. My siblings and I used to play a game to try and guess what was in the packages for days before Christmas.

My Godparents always bought me a gift. I felt very special this year! Their gift was a pretty blue dress trimmed with a thin plaid ribbon around the waist with a small bow. I was so excited, and thought it was just wonderful. What a pretty dress! I would feel so grown up when I wore that dress. I could not wait to wear it to church and to school. It was the one time I felt special. It was the only dress I had that came from a real store. The only dress I remembered that was not homemade or a hand-me-down from my sister. It was all mine – just for me – and I cherished it. That was the dress I would have on in the first picture I remember anyone taking of me. It was picture day at school, and I wore the blue dress. I combed my hair to the side and put a barrette in it. To this day, that is a picture I have kept. It remains in my little bag of memories, one of the few pictures that I have from my childhood.

It is always interesting how certain things resonate in our heads; which events stay, while others disappear from our consciousness. One particular afternoon, I had been thinking about not remembering much of my childhood. I was not quite sure why I did not have a recollection of growing up, and I began to wonder why.

HERE ARE GOD'S THOUGHTS THAT CAME THROUGH MY WRITING

Well, it is interesting how our minds work. We may conveniently forget —or is it GOD's intention that we do not, or cannot, remember until we can?

Well, let us ponder on that for a moment. Is it that we are unable to remember, or is it that our vision is blocked? Our pathway is unable to connect to the most painful experiences in our lives. Our soul may be on disconnect because there is a time and a place that we must reach in order to unlock the hidden emotions that surround our past.

Maybe God has switched our brain into survival mode to allow us to gain enough experience and knowledge to allow the perfect storm to send us those bolts of lightning, which will serve as enlightenment to our souls.

Well, let us ponder that for a moment. Well, maybe longer than a moment.

Our bodies and our souls may be intentionally on disconnect in some of our darkest moments as a survival technique, to shelter our physical being, because the trauma is so far beyond belief that we could never have seen the light in so much darkness.

The point is that things are darkest before the dawn. Awakening a soul is in the same vein: it is rarely moved to awaken, until something happens to begin the "Awakening."

A MESSAGE FROM GOD

May all who read this book understand that you were drawn to it on purpose. There is always a reason, and there is always a season in which your soul must no longer live in darkness, but must head towards the light. The yearning to walk in the truth becomes so overwhelming that you can no longer deny My purpose for you.

Let me say that again. "There comes a time when you can no longer deny My purpose for you. So, if you are here, please be present throughout your reading of this book – as maybe, just maybe, it is time to awaken your soul." Maybe it is time to awaken many souls at the same time – all at the same time. This has taken too long.

I must awaken the masses in warp speed to save humanity before it is too late.

So, this may truly be your time to walk in your truth, follow the direction of the light. It will lead one and all souls back to My door.

Isn't that the whole Truth and nothing but the Truth.

The clear intention of GOD is to bring all of his souls back to him!

He will show us the way. There is no doubt as to which way, once you begin your journey.

The journey, you say; the journey of a lifetime is to bring you back to My door.

So, let's begin by following a soul's journey!

We will start with this timid beautiful child – sweet, innocent, and so destined to begin an unforgettable path. A path that is forgotten until it is not!

Our lives and souls are all connected. As we move through our truths, we begin to see ourselves as individuals here on Earth set in our minds by man-made rules, by man-made concepts, of how we are supposed to think, act and be.

We cannot perceive anything but what we are taught, and the teachers are not teaching you what you need to know. They hide all of you from the truth as TRUTH IS LIGHT, TRUTH IS POWER, TRUTH WILL SET YOUR FREE – **AND**

If Truth will set you free then, "They will lose power."

Well, isn't that just as simple as can be? They will lose power as you gain yours.

Your soul's awakening will give you the power that has already been bestowed upon you. It is just waiting for you to claim it.

GOD EXPLAINS THE LITTLE GIRL

We need to look at that little girl. Here is her beginning.

She sits on an island waiting to bloom into a beautiful being. There is a path, on which others intervene and put her by herself in total seclusion and draw a bubble around her.

The older we get, the more we suppress. We become quite proficient at stopping our experiences from coming to the surface. We keep all those deep dark secrets hidden from the world and, by doing so, we step brick by brick down the pathway away from GOD, away from Truth, away from Light, away from the one thing, the one purpose: to be with GOD.

A bubble around her, you say. What does that mean? The membrane around her is impenetrable. No one can get through the bubble until she awakens and begins, little by little, to chip away at the bubble she is in until it begins to burst, one tiny bubble at a time.

It is 60-plus years inside the bubble. Let me say this loud and clear: the reason you were drawn to this book is that I cannot wait 60 years to awaken your soul. It must start now. Your journey must start NOW.

It takes a whole lifetime for some souls to break the bubble, so they are able to see and sit in the Truth.

Let us discover some of the things one's mind and soul connect on.

MEMORIES THAT CONNECT

We had a big garden. Mom worked in the garden with us during the summer. We canned green beans, carrots, yellow beans and other vegetables. In the fall we would go to the apple orchard and pick the dropped apples, bushels of them, load them in the car, and bring them home to make at least 100 quarts of apple sauce. The apples were cheaper to pick from the ground than picking off the tree, so that is what we did. It felt so good that Mom taught me how to help her, because she worked so hard. Then we would make apple pies all day and put them in the old stand-up freezer in the basement. We shined up the rest of the apples and gave them away at Halloween. Kids would come to the door and pick on us every year for giving out apples. We could not afford to give out candy bars. We would always try to go to houses that gave out candy, because that was a real treat for us.

In the fall, we would go to the butcher's market and get a side of beef. The butcher would cut it up in front of us and we would wrap the pieces in freezer paper and put the name of the cut on the paper in black magic marker and pack it in a cardboard box. Then, we would pack the boxes in the car and home we went to stack it in the freezer.

Mom was always cleaning the house and doing laundry. We helped her hang the laundry on the clothesline year-round. We only had an old-fashioned washing machine, with a spinner on the side, for a long time. Our home was always very clean. I used to help with vacuuming, washing, waxing, and buffing floors. I know my mother appreciated my sister and I helping her. We learned to do laundry and iron clothes at a very young age. We had to press the pleats down the back of the dress shirts just so; my Dad had to have perfectly pressed shirts every day, as did my older brothers, who worked at the local grocery store.

Mom taught my sister and I how to sew: first clothes for our dolls out of scraps, and then, to sew our own clothes. We learned to peel potatoes for mashed potatoes, always an enormous pan, almost every night. We still joke today that we really hate to peel potatoes and it is because we are all peeled out from our younger years.

One summer day, Dad said the house needed to be bleach-washed. He was sure the black spots on the white wood siding came from the wire factory smokestacks a couple blocks over from the house. I remember Mom going up on the ladder with the little bucket of bleach water and scrubbing and scrubbing every day. We tried to help Mom, but Dad came home yelling one night that the bush on the side of the house was dying because someone dropped bleach or paint on it. He was furious, and Mom said she would finish it herself. She worked on the siding for the longest time. I do not remember him ever helping, just inspecting and criticizing.

The neighbors would watch my mom working on the house, in the yard, mowing the lawn and planting the garden, but never said a word. Most of the neighbors' husbands worked at the factory and came home at 4 p.m. and took care of their houses, mowed their lawns, and did all the outside maintenance. However, my mom mowed the lawn for years with the push blade mower and did everything around the house. She was like a machine that never stopped and was never given any credit or acknowledgement from Dad.

One day there were these dump trucks delivering several loads of loam on the side yard, piles and piles. Well, no one sent a machine to spread this loam. We had a wheelbarrow and a shovel, and that was Mom's next job – as if taking care of six children, working in the garden, feeding the chickens and taking care of the house was not enough to keep her busy. We watched Mom, exhausted, shoveling loam into the wheelbarrow and pushing it up the slope and dumping it. She would sigh with exhaustion from time to time, but always very quietly. My older brothers would go out for a short time but would get tired after a load. Then Mom would go back, after she made us lunch, to toiling in the yard. I never saw the neighbors' wives working like my Mom.

She started her day very early, making Dad breakfast around 4:30 or 5 a.m., then waking us all and getting us ready for school. Dad left early every morning and came home very late at night, usually every day except Sunday. That was fine with us kids. We always felt better when he was not home. There was nothing he could do to us if he was not home, because Mom took care of us. She always cooked and kept the house clean, made our clothes, knitted and crocheted after dinner, and helped with our homework.

We were all expected to get good grades at school, be perfect in school, et cetera. Before Dad came home, Mom always washed her face and put her lipstick on – and yes, she was in her little house dress that they all wore back in the day.

The next memory that I have is playing in the back yard. Mom sent us out to rake leaves in the back corner of the yard, but we had a ball and were tossing it back and forth instead of raking, and guess who showed up early? We heard him bellow, "Get in here." My brother and I went running to the back door. He asked us, "What did your mother send you out to do?" We quietly replied, "rake leaves" and before we finished, his belt was off and he had my arm. He started to hit me across the backside. I began whaling and sobbing... he stopped! I could not believe it was only one powerful strike. Then, he reached for my brother. He hit him and he wrenched and squirmed, but refused to cry. I screamed, "Just cry, he will stop!" It was like he took some sick pleasure in causing pain, and then, seeing the welts and black and blue discolorations on our behinds and legs. This abuse went on for a long time. My brother refused to cry, and he hit him over and over, as I screamed. "Stop! Stop!" I do not know how many times he hit him, but he finally yelled and then, he stopped.

I am now in my 60s, just plain tired and feeling like life is just one day after the next, nothing very significant. The workdays come and go and the abuse from my childhood ruminates through my thoughts only to slip away into the darkness. Then reality comes back into focus, and I revert back to my work routine, realizing that I have had a lot of experience which has led to a successful career in business.

Everyone wants me to teach them the secrets to success in my current career, and many clients want me to wait to retire until they have completed their careers or established enough in their investing plans, so they are secure. That is, I guess, a measure of success that everyone likes to achieve. However, at some point we get tired, and it is just time to go in another direction or just plain have some fun. The continuation of many years of getting through each day just brings more of the same. The body is just worn down. Is there still meaning and purpose to what time there is left? Is it time to sit back and watch the rest of the world spin around running in all directions, in what seems like mean-ingless circles of drudgery?

There are always holidays to remind us of what it was to be younger: the house is filled with life again, even if just for a short time. But there is clearly something missing. It is not possible that your body and soul have nothing yet to do, nothing yet to accomplish. It is impossible to be here on Earth without a pur-pose or reason. If there were no reason or purpose, then we would not be.

So, then I started another journey, when all just seemed so dis-mal. It was March 1, 2020. My husband and I had just left my daughter's home. She was not well and had to be hospitalized for some testing. As we head towards home, approximately an hour into our 7-hour drive, the phone rings. "Mom" – with hesitation in his voice, my youngest says – "There has been a terrible accident. He is really bad. You need to get to the hospital, as soon as possible. He was flown by Lifestar to a Critical Care Unit in a large hospital. They don't know if he will make it." At that point, I was driving and not much else registered. I told him, "We are on our way, and tell him we will be there as soon as we can." My hands were glued to the steering wheel. I just stared forward and drove for several hours, unable to speak or stop. My husband kept saying, "Please stop and I'll drive," but I am not sure what he said even registered with me. After several hours I looked up at him and said, "I need to stop. I have to stop." We turned off at the next rest area. We switched seats and he drove the rest of the way back home, directly to the hospital. We parked and rushed in, up the elevator and down the corridor, one of the longest walks a mother could ever have to take.

Upon our arrival, my younger son came to me to tell me it would be very difficult to see. I just needed to go directly to him; it was worse than I ever could have imagined. His lifeless body was attached to so many machines, with two nursing staff and multiple doctors constantly by his side. As I approached his bed, I knew this would be the most difficult battle of his life. The tears rolled down my face as the doctors spoke about his injuries. Each injury by itself was life threatening, and the list went on and on. The hope was to stabilize him, for now. They really could not do any more for him until they could stabilize him. And so the journey began, as each and every moment was critical, each breath might be his last.

This is the young man who was born when I was just a child. He was a beautiful baby. He was extremely smart, tested genius several times over the years, had big blue eyes and curly blonde hair, and the perfect smile and a robust laugh that was just infectious. I could not understand why he was always in pain, wrenching when he drank his formula, crying out in pain. The doctors changed his formula so many times. I ended up giving him canned milk with Karo syrup as a last resort. His world was filled with allergies. One doctor after another, many looked at a young mother with condescending eyes, as though you somehow caused your child to have food and environmental sensitivities. Years of doctor visits, altering diets, asthma, migraine headaches and vomiting persisted. I made countless visits to the school explaining what his issues and allergies were to so many people who just had no idea and thought it was all made up. My son was different. He had so many problems with his digestion, diet, headaches – you name it. There was a time we thought he had cancer, as his weight loss was so drastic that he lost over 10 pounds in just a few weeks, and he was only about 70 pounds at the time. I always felt like I was living on the edge waiting for the next thing that would make him sick. I finally met a wonderful pediatrician, who was so supportive. This doctor actually studied children's allergies and became well-known for his practice as a pediatric allergist. He taught me so much; as he studied, he would give me his books to read, and we would discuss them as I went through them. I was eventually named his practice's "Allergy Mom." He would have distressed mothers call me for support from time to time. We would discuss how to deal with the diets, behavioral issues, all the children's school issues and how to explain to the parents of your children's friends what to do if they had a problem when they were not at home.

One day the doctor asked, "Where is your son's father?" I just smiled; there were many people who asked if my children had a father. He was just never present for doctor visits, church, school functions, practices, games or any social events, teacher conferences, you name it. There were many years of 2 or 3 visits to the doctor's office a week with our children, and the doctor never met my children's father. On one occasion, when my son was admitted to the hospital, his father showed up for a few minutes and I introduced him to the doctor. I should have mentioned, we were married and lived together for about 17 years and had three children. He was one of those dissociated fathers, who did not think it was his responsibility to help care for his children, his wife, or be involved in anything that we did. My favorite saying back then was, "I was a married, single mother of three," who ran my own business, as well as assisting the running of a business for someone who did not give a damn about me or our kids.

All these things were passing through my mind as my oldest son lay lifeless in the hospital bed. His father showed up and looked at me as if somehow, I might be able to fix this. The guilt in his eyes and his demeanor were unbearable to me. He looked so defeated, so lost, like a fragile little child. As I heard what was going on it seemed as though somehow, he was looking for me to console him or somehow ease his consciousness for what had happened to our son; wonders never cease.

I could not spend any of my emotional energy on him at that point. There was nothing to say. Things are what they are, and at some point, you have to just accept what had been and no longer linger in that space.

My feelings were scattered, and I began to think of the years that my son and I had after we had gotten back on track. Our conversations about life, what happened in his life and how sorry he was for what had gone on between us after his parents' divorce. How sorry he was for listening to all the awful things he heard from his paternal grandfather and his father. How he understood why I felt the way I did and why I had to leave. He knew just how I felt, but did not realize it until he stepped away from that world and realized how toxic it was. All these conversations about what he wished he had done, and how he wished he had done things differently, were swirling through my head. He told me many times he wanted to be the son I wanted, the one with the family and to be successful, but just felt like he could not do it. He loved his sister and brother, and all his nieces and nephews, and they all loved him and looked up to him. He lived his life like an eagle soaring through the trees. He was certainly the daredevil kind of guy. He was so energetic, so full of life, and always the life of the party.

As I reached for his hand, I felt that energy of connection, that special bond with him that only a mother can have. I felt the energy flow from my hand to his. I knew, in that moment, he felt my presence with him. A child can always feel the presence of the parent, the one who is the constant, the caregiver and the one their children can always come to when things are down – no judgment, just open arms and a place of safety, even when they are adults. "It is always good to talk to Mom," he would tell me. A mother provides a safe place and space that no one else can. I think there is a grounding that takes place when the anchor in your life is just there to listen and be.

After the divorce, his father and grandfather turned him against me with all their evil hatred, never understanding that I could no longer survive in the prison they built around me and my children. They never thought I would have the strength to leave, especially after the constant threats about taking my kids over the years. It took some time, years, for my oldest son to realize that the one who truly loved him no matter what was Mom. He said it many times during his last few years and many times during his extended stays with me. I just wanted to tell him one more time how much I loved him.

There was only my son and myself and the clicking of the machines, clicking over and over again, as I prayed that he would recover, and we would start over somewhere new. I would take him away from all the terrible things that happened to him. I prayed and prayed but as the days passed the Critical Care doctors, whom we had meetings with periodically, kept getting more and more difficult to handle. The updates were not really any better, as each day turned into night. It was one step forward and two steps back. It seemed like a roller coaster that just would not stop. The darkness was closing in as each hour and day passed. The surgeries were numerous, and each seemed critical, as they tried to save his life. Each procedure was performed with precision and exact execution, but there was always that knowledge that whatever the outcome was, he would never be the same.

I studied on my phone about traumatic brain injuries, spinal injuries, neck, back, ribcage, leg wounds and more. The doctors would engage in conversations with me on all these topics throughout his hospitalization. The head Critical Care doctor walked with me to his room one time, and asked, how they were doing according to what I was reading. I told them I was not second guessing them. I just needed to know what the next steps were and understand their terminology, as they were talking with me. He was a very caring doctor, no arrogance or condescension in his demeanor. I think he was just trying to make conversation to see how I was holding up. He recommended that I try to get some sleep, maybe go home for a night and come back in the morning. He spoke of me needing my strength for the next few days to come. He did convince me to go home for one night. I remember waking late the next afternoon in a panic about how long I slept. Back to the hospital I went.

The doctors knew I was struggling to keep up with all the different surgeries and terms they were using. However, they were amazed that I was able to follow as closely as I did. "Surely," I said to the head doctor one day, "this is not an education that any parent ever wants, especially under these circumstances." I prayed day and night for the strength to make the right decisions. I prayed for all the doctors and nurses that were in his unit. I wanted to do what was best for my son and work together with all the people who were working around the clock to save him.

The days turned into a week, and then, into two weeks. The time passed second by second as our family watched the clock of his life tick away. The doctors held meeting after meeting, trying to determine the best course of action, but as time slipped by, there was no denying that the very serious discussions were no longer able to be put off. There was so much to review and so much to understand.

One of the last surgeries was just so critical that the surgeon was called in around 10 p.m. because waiting was not an option. The pressure in his brain was so high, they just could not wait any longer. They had to remove part of his skull to allow the brain to swell or he would not make it. The surgery was over at around 3 a.m. A very special nurse had begged the surgeon to talk to me when he was done, not to send someone else as he usually does, but to please speak to me himself. She told him I would not leave my son's side and I was someone he would be able to speak to easily.

The surgeon was exhausted as he strolled into the family waiting area and approached me. He asked if that was my son he had just performed surgery on, and I said, "Yes, he is." He sat with me for some time and explained that the nurse had asked him, actually begged him to speak with me. I asked, "Are you the actual surgeon? Everyone told me that you do not speak to family members." He said he was the surgeon, and he does not speak to family, as he does not have a very good personality for talking to families. I smiled and thanked him for coming to see me. We talked and he explained the surgery to me in great detail. We discussed his options moving forward. The situation was not promising, but he did tell me that if they needed him to come back and perform the final surgery, I had nothing to worry about. He would make sure he did it himself. I was so grateful for the opportunity to speak to him and when we finished, he looked up at me and said, "I am very hungry. I need to go home and eat dinner. They called me right as I was sitting down to eat but told me I needed to get to the hospital as soon as I could." I thanked him again, and he slowly stood up, and ever so softly said, "good night" and sauntered to the door.

Everyone kept saying how strong my son was, yet we still needed one more test to see whether the brain damage had split the two hemispheres, or if the connective tissue between the lobes was still intact. If it was intact, then he stood a good chance that with some intensive long-term rehabilitation, he may be able to function at some level. He might be able to communicate. Possibly, be able to walk and talk, but they also said he will never be the son you remembered. They stressed that "he would never be the man you all remembered."

Finally, I spoke to my son through a medium and in his own unique style, he let me know that he would try very hard to be able to get the last test they needed, but if the results showed he was damaged beyond repair, that we must listen to the doctors and let him go. This was on my mind, for we had spoken of this many times, to never keep him alive with a machine. If he was just going to lie in a bed for people to come see him and feel bad that he was a vegetable, please let him go. He communicated that he knew that the three people who truly loved him all his life were Mom, his Grandma (my mother) and his sister.

As he indicated to me, he put all his strength into his being, to allow the one last test to be done. Waiting for the results was excruciating torture. The test results were not good, the prayers began to change as hope dwindled. I begged God to help us all make the right decision.

A few more days passed, eventually he was the longest patient to stay in the critical care unit. Many others had come and gone. Some were transferred to other facilities, and some did not make it. The day for making the decision had come. They could no longer keep him on all the machines. There was no brain activity. The doctors called a family conference. He was disconnected from all the support systems later that day, but like in his own unique style, as he always did, things were going to happen on his time. He chose to stay with us a while longer. I sat by his side and held his hand all night in his room by myself, a mother and son waiting for GOD. I talked to him, I prayed and just listened to him breathe over and over, every breath was a struggle. Throughout the time he was there, there were many signs all around us, but it was very difficult to see them when things were happening.

Morning came and I had to call the family and, as the others came in, I knew he was not going to be with us much longer. I held his hand and, as he took his last breath, a massive flock of birds did three huge circles in front of the window of his hospital room. Two birds stayed behind and flittered around for a few moments, then flew off toward the sky together. He had told me that his Grandma had been with him the whole time, through the medium a week or so earlier, and I truly believe she came for his soul, and they are together now. They soared up to the sky together and so it would have to be the two of them for now...together for now.

THEY WILL WAIT. THEY WILL WATCH FROM ABOVE.

THEY WILL BE PATIENT.

A MOTHER'S PAIN ONLY INTENSIFIES WITH TIME

The total and complete void a parent feels after losing a child is indescribable. The emptiness inside your being, like your entire heart is no longer in your body, complete and utter despair, waiting and knowing that here lies before you only the earthly part of your beloved child, the child you made sure was not given away. The child whose life had changed your life forever. The child who had given you a purpose in life, a reason to live, a reason to stay in a miserable situation until you could not stay any longer. He is gone and you are left with your thoughts, knowing GOD has called him, knowing you will never again have those heartfelt conversations, see that magnificent smile and those dancing blue eyes, or hear the sound of that laugh, the laugh that only he had.

All these things whirling and rushing through my head made me dizzy. I had to sit down; I no longer had the strength to stand on my feet. How long can I do this? It was so hard to breathe, and the air was not going into my body. I felt so weak and light-headed. How could I survive this? How could I go on? I just needed to breathe. I needed air in my lungs. I seemed to be in a dream. This surely could not be real. Maybe I would wake up, and it was only a horrific dream. I looked around and everyone in the room was crying; it was real. It was happening. He was gone.

Days turned into weeks, and weeks turned into months. The pain was so real, so excruciating, each and every moment, just consuming my every thought. I could not get out of bed in the morning. I did not want to talk, did not want to eat and did not want to face anyone. No church services were available as this was during COVID. How do you bring closure? Waiting for the two weeks to slow the spread turned into months, and we still could not have a service. Looking at the ashes every day and feeling total despair.

Surely, this could not be all that there is. Somehow there had to be closure. The movie reels played in my dreams at night. The old-fashioned movie reels with the tapes, as his life would start, and I would watch him running to me with open arms as a baby and see all the wonderful things that happened in his life. Then, as abruptly, as it began the tapes snapped and the reel went round and round. It clicked each time the end of the tape hit the projector...click...click...click. The end of the story, the end of my child, he was gone, just like that. Gone before it was his time. Gone from this Earth way too soon. I would wake up in a panic lying in a pool of cold sweat, just weeping for what could have been. Eventually, we had a very private immediate-family service for him. It was not what we would have done under other circumstances. There had to be something that would help me get up in the morning, but going to work would take time.

I tried to read books on grief recommended by a friend who was a therapist, and tried to talk to a few people, but it was not helping. I turned to GOD once more, praying for the strength to go on for my husband, my children, and my grandchildren's sakes. I needed to do something for me. I felt like I needed to change something in my life. There could not be just despair and sadness for the rest of my life. This was not fair to all around me to have lost him, and then to lose me to total despair as well. I was debilitated, completely sullen, exhausted, and trying to figure out how to go on. I had to find a way; I had to come back to life for all of them.

My daughter had been ill as well, and was struggling with many symptoms that were not being identified by traditional medicine. We began a journey together which also led to my own journey. Anything that we decided to do became a marathon mission for both of us.

I started my journey with a holistic approach. I became the celery juicing queen using the protocols from a very famous author and podcaster Anthony Williams, also known as the Medical Medium. I spent about a year using his methods and slowly but surely made progress, both physically and mentally. I was back to work and starting to feel like I was alive again.

That entire path kept me going another 6 months or so, but I still was not right. My body had been through so much. I was not sure what was missing. I decided to go to a holistic wellness center and have an evaluation done. Low and behold, there were a lot of things going on, both physically and emotionally.

Many physical things were identified, and I began a regiment of recommended supplements. I was holding back the death of my son and all the pain of my divorce when talking to this holistic practitioner. I suppose I did not think it was relevant at the time.

They were able to slowly remove many toxins from my body, which seemed to help me move to the next level. I was taking one round of supplements and then another, each taking its own time do its magic and clear my body.

At some point, we had to get to the underlying issues of my stress and deep pain. This is where the real work came into the picture. I finally admitted, out loud, that I had lost my son, and this was very difficult to talk about. I mentioned how he had struggled all his life, and how I felt I did all I could, but it just was not enough. I felt that if this had not happened, then things may have been different. Maybe if I had stayed in my miserable marriage, things may have been different for him. I wanted so desperately to help him, but ultimately the end result was not for me to choose. The end result was GOD's will, not mine. Those thoughts went on and on. I seemed to be blaming myself for all that was, for all that happened, similar to what I had done as a child. It appeared to be a theme throughout my life. I was always taking the blame, guilt and shame of every event that happened all around me and those I loved.

The practitioner looked at me and spoke. "So, I wondered how long it would take for you to tell me what was really bothering you – but we are here now so let's talk about all of that."

Here – right here – is where it got so real. I knew something big would have to happen to help me with the great sadness that had taken over my life.

I had gone to church all my life as a devout Catholic, and brought my children up in the Church. I even spent many years working with teenagers and teaching religion classes, while my kids were in junior and senior high school. Even though I was a single mom, I spent as much time as possible trying to be involved with activities that kept me near my children and their friends. I enjoyed working with the kids and enjoyed the teenagers. They were always so energetic and fun to hang out with. I formed many bonds with different children over the years and still feel close to many of them to this day.

Acknowledging your fears and doubts to someone out loud can be very difficult. Strong people do not like to show or discuss their vulnerabilities with anyone – or admit that they are actually human. Also, we do not want to acknowledge that we may not have all the answers, or that we may not have always made the best choices for ourselves or others. As I began to explore some of the feelings I had in my appointments with the wellness practitioner, she began to open my eyes to many new revelations. I had actually blocked out a lot of things as a child that became more and more evident as time went on.

This was truly a time of self-discovery for me. At the same time that I was seeing this holistic group, I also was reunited with a very lovely lady from my past. She was a very kind soul, an energy healer and medium, who I had known for years. My initial encounters with her were very lighthearted. However, after my son passed, I saw her at an event, and she began speaking about my son. He was coming to her trying to tell her he wanted a birthday party and for us to celebrate him, and the funny thing was it was right before his birthday. He kept showing her a birthday cake with candles. He kept telling her he did not want me to be sad, that he was fine. He sent several messages to me that day, and I was so grateful for seeing this woman. I eventually set up several appointments with her for energy healing; I really wanted to talk to my mom on the other side, as well as my son. This led me further down the path on my journey.

There was a sense of knowing that healers had been placed on my path for a reason. They did not just appear, they appeared because it was time for me to awaken to the Truth – and the Truth began to flow like a river, slowly at first, and then the flood gates opened and there was no stopping the Truth from coming to light.

The coming days and months revealed so much that it was extremely hard to process. Could there possibly have been this much that I had buried from my past? Was it possible that all these things were my real story, that story that I locked up in that box so no one would ever find out? How long could I continue to deny the Truth? How long could I continue to bury all of this and pretend it did not happen? How long?

I continued to work on myself and began to realize that there were so many times where the truth had been revealed, but I refused to acknowledge it. So many times, that confirmation of events had been placed in front of me, but I chose to ignore and deny it. It was just too painful, just too much. All of it was just too much.

If I had accepted and allowed myself to believe it, my whole life would have been turned upside down. The fantasy world I had made up in my mind to protect my past from surfacing would have to be let go and replaced with this very painful realization that my life was very dark. There were so many painful things buried in my past. That was not something that I wanted to accept, not when it happened and certainly not now. I thought it is not so bad going through life with blinders on trying to make believe all is well, when it certainly was far from well!

Finding the truth in our lives, admitting what has happened in the past, realizing what was in our past and accepting it for what it was is part of the process. Knowing that we cannot change the past, but acknowledging it, is a paramount first step to understanding ourselves and our soul, and the purpose of all that is and finally finding meaning and healing.

When we are not ready to see the truth, it cannot be seen. When we are not ready to believe the truth, then it does not come to us. When we refuse to accept the truth, then denial takes over our thoughts. We will not believe the truth.

THE BEGINNING OF THE TRUE STORY

He came home from work, and his usual stop at the bar, and he was angry. He was drunk. He forced himself on her as he had so many times. It certainly was not a loving consensual relationship. She never thought he would treat her like this, he had been nice to her when they dated. She wept in bed all night. That became number five. Oh. That little girl in the bubble, here was her true beginning. There was no doubt, that it would be another child – number five. This had happened before. He felt entitled. She was powerless to hold him back when he was in this state. That is what she thought back then.

So, that became the little girl in the bubble. He was so angry. He did not want another child. How could she get pregnant? Yet again, how could she be pregnant? It was just one night. He knew it was wrong, what he did to his wife – but he did it anyway, because he could. He did it anyway, because he wanted power. He did it anyway, because he could show her he was in control.

And so, he went to church, to pray away the deed. But that baby came anyway. The thoughts of his actions began to resonate in his mind, bothering him ever so slightly.

This is only one of many victims in his life. He just took whatever he wanted. Anywhere, anytime, he felt important, and his ego overtook his senses. More and more victims fell to his cruelty.

It was not bad enough that he abused his wife. He also abused, all the other vulnerable women around him. After all, he had moved onto a very interesting job in the big city with some very high-powered individuals who had total disregard for human life. When anyone got in their way, things were handled immediately and ruthlessly.

He felt entitled to abuse all that crossed his path and when he was angry or drunk it did not matter who that was. He lashed out at everyone in his path including his wife. It did not stop there – how could it? His cruelty knew no bounds. The ultimate cruelty came at home – after his wife, it was his children, and here was number five.

Born in the Blizzard of 1958, is the memory that cannot escape him. How ironic was this? Conceived in turmoil and delivered in turmoil and so it went, a life embroiled in turmoil. There was no one to protect that infant child. Everyone around her, outside her bubble was fighting for survival. When he came home from work, there was hell to pay by anyone who would get in his way. His wife was frightened; her parents had left this world, no one to protect or help her. Now there were five children, and they were all deathly afraid of him, as well.

Mom always said after four children it was just more of the same. Now, I think how desperate she must have been to stay with this man. How fearful and abused she really was.

He walked through the door, and we all had to make ourselves scarce, so we did not upset him. Mom tried to protect us from his wrath. Sometimes it worked, but kids will be kids. And talking and laughing was enough to set his rage in motion. We were sent away from the dinner table for talking and laughing. We were sent to bed hungry, and then, he was gone early in the morning. Mom would feed us, and then send us off to school.

I remember the first day of kindergarten, Mom walked me down the sidewalk and when I saw the main doors, I wanted to run to those doors. Mom wanted to walk me to my classroom, but I said, "No. I can do it." I squirmed out of her hand and headed down the hallway with a purpose. Was it to create a new world or escape the one I was living in at home?

Be a good girl. Help your mother, dust, vacuum and do the laundry. Do the dishes. Wax the floors. Iron the shirts. This is what the girls were taught. Keep the house clean. Keep up the yard. Stay out of Dad's way. So, this little girl just wanted to be loved. She did it all, everything she was told or asked to do, but there was no affection. There was no one who could offer true love and compassion. All the people in her family were just trying their best to survive. How can anyone show caring, love, or compassion when they are all in survival mode? It was literally every man for himself in that home, and so the soul of this little girl was pushed deeper and deeper into the darkness, there was just darkness. How does one escape from the darkness?

It envelops you. It becomes an everlasting struggle to find an alternative world – another place where you can be without that darkness, without the pain of the truth swallowing you whole, trying to find a crack in the bubble that keeps you in the darkness always.

I wanted friends. I wanted to help others who were afraid. Maybe we could help each other not be afraid. I was everyone's friend, but never felt like I had any true friends. I could not have friends to my house like other kids did. Mom always said we have too many of our own children, so no one was allowed to come over. No one was allowed to come to our home unless they played in the yard, and they had to stay outside all the time. I begged and pleaded to have my friends over, but it never happened. It was hard to keep friends when everyone kept going over each other's homes, but I could not. So, the isolation continued: even though I was friends with everyone, I truly had no real, close friends.

Child number six was born four years after me. He never stood a chance at having a fair shake in life. My heart went out to him. I often thought: there's no one to help him, but what about me? I had to get away from this cruel, overbearing father. We need to teach him how to stay out of the way. I had to stay out of the way.

It was always scary when Dad was home. He never seemed to be happy about anything. He was always irritated by anything we asked him. It always seemed like he would just be angry. He was nice on the phone to others, then it was like a switch flipping in him, back to angry when he addressed any of us.

Going to the grocery store was a major event. I remember going to the grocery store with Mom. It was one thing that made me feel special. It was the only time I could be alone with Mom. Little did I know what she was going through at the time; I was just a child.

Sunday dinners were quite important in our house. Mom sang in the choir, until dad made a big deal out of her coming home from mass 30 minutes later than if she had not been singing, which meant dinner was 12:30 p.m. instead of 12 p.m. He insisted she had to quit singing in the choir. One thing at a time, he took it all; everything, all of it. All her joy removed one thing at a time, until she had nothing left that brought her happiness. I remember feeling so bad that Mom would not sing anymore. She had such a beautiful voice.

It was all about control. I never made the connection as a child, though I knew it was not nice to make her quit. The most beautiful voice I had ever heard. She sang like an angel, such a lovely voice. Many years later people would continue to comment about what a lovely voice she had and how they missed her singing at church. After that, I cannot remember her ever singing in front of my father again. She would sing to us sometimes, when he was not around or at the house, as she was doing her work, but never again in front of him.

Even in her later years when she would go to church, she would not sing for him. That must have been part of her stubborn streak, that she would never give him the pleasure of hearing her sing again as long as she lived. She stuck to that until the day she died. She was 95 when she passed. That was some long grudge to keep.

THE BOX WITH THE BIG LOCK

We will go back and forth, as your childhood experiences are a combination of what was and what is.

The little girl is independent; she has a strength from within, where she has blocked out all that torture and all that pain. She does not want to know, not today, not before, not when it happened.

So, she put it in a box and sealed it shut. She made sure no one could get inside. She locked it with a big lock and buried the key somewhere no one could find it.

In doing this, she protected herself from being found out. What if someone knew? What if someone found out? What would happen to her? Would they send her away? Would she ever see her family? What exactly would happen if someone found out?

She did not know. Just the fact that it happened, she knew it was bad, but how bad? Is that real? Is that what happens to others? She would not ask because she did not know. It was all very confusing to her. Just hide it. Hide it!

None of this was good. Do not tell. They may get rid of you! Do not tell your friends. Do not tell your sister – she cannot help. When she tried, he hurt her. No one can help! Just be quiet. Stay quiet!

Hopefully no one will notice, and you can stay, because where else could you go? The fear, the pain, the shame that you may have done something wrong is too risky. Do not risk them putting you out on the street with no one to care for you.

Make all of it go away and maybe, just maybe, it will keep you safe. Help Mom, please your Mom, and maybe she will not get rid of you. After all, your brothers told you, "You were adopted." Remember, you are not one of them. So, they can just get rid of you, no one really cares about you. No one really notices you, so, be good, be a good girl and pray to GOD that they do not get rid of you.

Lock up the key to the sins and no one will find out. I hope no one will find out. I pray no one will find out.

THE BEATINGS

Dad was really angry. Both my brother and I wet the bed again. He was so angry that he set up a folding cot in the laundry/dining room with no door. He made us sleep together so that if we wet the bed, we would wet each other and none of the rest of the beds would get ruined. Sunday morning, when Dad was home, he would make my brother and I get a switch from the woods behind our house and bring it inside and place it under our bed in preparation for the next event. It seemed like some sick ritual. He actually seemed to take pleasure in watching us wrench in pain. If we wet the bed, we had to bring him the stick, with only our underwear on, in the living room and he would hit us with the stick until we were screaming in pain. Our mother could not watch when he was in such a rage. Many times we had welts, other times black and blue discolorations, and sometimes we got a little bloody. I would wear pants under my dress to go to church after the beatings, so when we sat on the wooden benches my legs would not stick to the varnished wood. I learned that early on, you only needed your bruised legs to stick to that varnished wood bench once and then, get pulled off by your father for not standing fast enough. Oh, that was excruciating and made me tremble and quiver in pain. Sometimes just trying to sit at the table for breakfast was too much. He seemed to relish watching us while we wrenched in pain, and he made us sit down, quietly of course.

All of this treatment caused more fear and exacerbated the situation. I think we kept wetting the bed because we were so scared, always remembering how he would hurt us over and over again. That never seemed to work very well. I guess Dad thought we would stop wetting our bed if he hit us hard enough. I do remember going to the doctor and my mother asking why we were wetting our beds; the doctor said we probably had weak bladders and not to worry, we would grow out of it.

One day my brother and I had to get new sticks and we decided to get really dry sticks that would break when he hit us. Seemed like a good idea at the time. We just did not want to get hurt anymore. Well, you can imagine how that worked out. Definitely not good when we giggled because the stick broke. We never tried that again. We could not sit for days.

Then, the infamous talk from back in the day. You do not discuss anything outside this home. What happens here is family business and you will not discuss anything that goes on in this house with anyone. Do you understand? No one!

Eventually, I was moved into a room with a double bed with my sister. My older brothers would try to scare me and told me there was an electric buzzer in the bed. They told me that if I peed the bed, I would get an electric shock. They would wait until I went to bed and stand outside my bedroom door taunting me, "Do not wet your bed or you will get the BUZZZZ." They would just laugh as I cried myself to sleep.

I guess when these are the types of things you do remember, one must ask, "What is it that you cannot remember?" I certainly cannot remember anyone ever telling me I did a good job or anyone saying I was a good kid. That was for sure.

IT CAME FROM ALL DIRECTIONS

The cruelty came out of nowhere. Some days we just stayed out of the way, and we were okay. Sometimes we hid, so Dad did not see us. Sometimes we could not find a place to hide.

Do not get loud when Dad comes home. Make sure you do your chores and do a good job. Do not get in trouble in school; get your homework done and get good grades. Dad had no sense of humor when it came to grades. Mom always helped with homework. She walked around the table and helped when we were stuck, round and round the table, where we all sat together to do our homework each night after school.

MY MESSAGES FROM GOD CAME IN THE MIDDLE OF THE NIGHT

There is so much to do. I am watching, and things are not going in the right direction. I know you feel it. It is time to move through some important things. The real problems are that those, who should be paying attention, are not. People have become complacent just letting themselves be led by others, so they do not have to use critical thinking. We need to finish waking the masses. They are all in a trance, a coma of sorts. It is time to wake them all up. Let them know man has gotten lazy and is trying to take the easy way out.

The wealthy and the rulers throughout the world have taken away your right to free will, by dictating what you can and cannot do. Technology is out of control: without free will humankind will not advance. You will be stuck in a slave state for centuries. But it is not too late to change course. It is all up to you, I mean up to mankind. But you must choose freedom and free will.

The elites have too much power over individuals. They have become the arbiters of UNTRUTH trying to pass it along as truth. Nothing they say is truth, not even close to truth – not even close. They must change their direction immediately, or they must be replaced with others who will speak the truth. Change is coming one way or another.

I have given you free will, but it must be exercised, and it is not. Man has gotten lazy in your world. Busy doing much to do about nothing, chasing wealth, power and control, not paying attention to what is important.

The Evolution of Souls. Each must do their part to save the world. Start thinking for yourselves; stop following the masses. They are not leading you to the truth. I will say it again. All you are being told is just to control you and stop free thinking. When people lead with Love, then change just happens. They are leading through fear and that is not how it should be. Man must not live in fear. To live in fear is to live in virtual prison. You will no longer live in fear, when you have learned to trust Me. They must all learn to trust Me. For I am the Truth, the Light, and the Way. The Only Way.

There are many in the world who will lead the change from everywhere. It is already happening. The time is here to stand up to tyranny and move mankind forward. It has taken too long. For many elites of the world have gained immense power and it is not to be. There are many throughout the world and others will fall, the Truth always prevails. But free will keeps getting in the way. Many have accepted that they will need to die to show the world this is not so, but many will see the truth.

Do not follow the media, as it has all been a lie. You must follow the truth. GOD will lead the way, but you must choose truth. Do not be confused: there is a path for all, but they must seek truth their own truth. We are the Champions of the world. Love and Truth, two very basic concepts, yet so many miss the point.

It is getting harder and harder to deny the Truth. Everything you are being fed is a lie; there is only Love and Truth. In the end, love and truth will prevail. It will have to be in the end, because love and truth will prevail. I will show you. Many throughout the world will die, for it is the only way for love and truth to prevail.

Take your place and we will expose it all day by day.

Living your truth is the first step. The step I need you to make. It is not as hard as you think. You are practicing your gifts on a few. Soon, it will be used to lead the masses to light.

I will light up the world like an electric switch and you will have your plan, you will help the people. It is so. You will not fear, you will know it to be. Now, today must be as it is, go and learn as you must. You are being guided to continue your journey. For yours will make a difference. This is always what you wanted: to make a difference.

So, let us march on.

Learn the skills, learn the truth, as it will set you free. Do not lose the faith. Do not get off course.

Learning the patience to stay the course has been a big lesson. But you have finally gotten it. Stay with me. Stay the course. The message will come, and I will guide you. Sail away, sail away, sail away with me. I like that too; it is just more like a journey. Let us go. Time to go!

ANOTHER MEMORY LOCKED IN THE BOX

I am cowering in the corner. It is just a hard place.

I am playing and he pushes me in the street; not carefully, either. "Pick me up. Do not leave me on the ground, please." "Things are left here – do you want to be left here?" – "Take me with you Dad, do not leave me... Pick me up." My knees are bleeding, my stockings are ripped, and my hands are scraped. He did not want to get his suit dirty. So, I had to get up myself. I am crying and I follow him, then get into the car. He yells at me to stop crying, or else. I whimper and try to stop, but he gets mad and hits me again. I am crying louder now. If he would just stop hitting me, I could stop crying. Go away, go away – leave me alone. I just cry more and more. Why did he hit me? It was not my fault. Why did he do it? We got home and I ran to Mom. She cleaned me up and sent me to bed. They fought and Dad yelled, but I did not know what he said. He yelled and Mom told him to keep his voice down. He was angry and she went to her room crying.

Mom came to see me later. She asked me what happened. I told her he pushed me to the ground, that is how I got hurt. He shoved me down with his foot. I yelled "Please help me," but there was not anyone there to help me. I said, "Do not hurt me," but he did not care.

I had the blue dress on; the one that came from my godparents for Christmas. It was ripped when I fell to the ground. I liked my dress. It was a nice dress, but it was ruined. I cried for my little blue dress. I was mad he ruined my dress. I was so proud of that dress. I hated him for ruining my dress. It made me sad and I cried.

Mom made me a new dress, but it was not like my blue dress. I was five, and my blue dress was special. I felt special in that dress.

Dad came to see me. I told him, "I do not like you. Stay away from me." He bellowed, "You can go to bed with no supper." I did not care. He was just mean to me. I knew Mom would feed me when he was gone. So I cried myself to sleep.

Now, I wonder if he broke her ribcage on purpose. It happened more than once. Mom tried to appease him. He was angry so often. It was hard for her to read him; anger always took over. She would cook for him at all hours of the night. He demanded she wait on him hand and foot. He demanded; he would not cook for himself. She had to get up and cook for him no matter what time he showed up and cook an entire meal for him. He was entitled and she complied to keep the peace. It was a nightmare if he was not treated like a king. Every once in a while, he would throw her a bone and she was supposed to be grateful to him, like it was some big deal. She had nothing. She saved pennies and ran the house like clockwork because she had no choice. He had his shiny shoes, his fancy suits, and his perfectly pressed shirts all in a row in his closet. His suits went to the dry cleaner and were always perfect.

Mom had nothing, she wore worn out little house dresses and put her lipstick on when he came home; she had to greet him at the door every time he came home. It was hard after her parents were gone. She was all alone. Working, ironing, cleaning, she ran that house, as her mom would say, "like a top," always keeping it perfectly clean, every task executed with precision. Dad would not have it any other way. She worked in the garden, the kitchen, the yard and more until she was exhausted; she worked like a dog, but he did not even notice.

They dropped loads of dirt in the yard, and she moved it all over the yard, in the terrible heat, one wheelbarrow at a time, she shoveled like a mule by herself, while he was out drinking and fooling around with women all over. He was a real Casanova – or so he thought.

She toiled in the garden, worked in the yard, hung laundry on the clothesline, and on and on. She tried to get help from our church, but the Priest just sent her home to go back to do more of the same, more abuse; more cruelty. She was so unhappy. She tried so hard. She took care of everything.

Then, there was the undeniable, right in front of her eyes – right over the stone wall. Her husband slapped her with the undeniable truth looking her in the eyes every single day. What could she do? How could she go on? It went from bad in the beginning, to worse and worse. Dad's sister did not want to hear it. She had to work every day outside of the house to get by. Dad made more money than her husband. Mom should not complain. She was able to stay home. At least her brother made enough money for his wife to stay home. Mom could not talk to her anymore.

She could not talk to anyone. They were all struggling with their own families. Dad's older brother was beating his wife in a drunken state, younger brother and his wife were always fighting, and both of them were alcoholics. His middle sister was not emotionally well, and his youngest sister was always on medication and out of sorts, most times, making very little sense. There was no one to talk to. Mom was left to suffer in silence with no one to turn to, no one who would acknowledge her abuse by her husband or her children's abuse at the hands of their father.

His anger was explosive. He did not like us making noise when he was around. We had to just sit quietly.

He was cruel to everyone he came in contact with. He loved the power that came with his connections at work – there was no doubt. He had the ability to hurt anyone he wanted. If he got angry, he just lashed out at anyone who stepped in his path, including our poor Mom. She learned to stay out of his way early on. But sometimes, that did not matter. He was just despicable, especially when he was drunk. Help and hope were gone, just despair remained. Learning how to survive, that was the only thought, how to make it through the night. She cried herself to sleep many nights, not knowing where to turn.

His own mother knew how cruel he was but he made money, so she never protected Mom. She could not protect herself or her children from her husband. She had to live with it and Mom would have to live with it as well.

There was no compassion in Dad's family, either. All the boys were hateful just like their father. The oldest sister is angry like her brothers, and so it goes on and on. Everyone suffered in silence. No one talked about it and if they did there was hell to pay. Silence was a requirement for the abuse to continue, for it to move from one generation to the next.

The priests drank because they knew about all the abuse and could not get away from the Truth. The Truth was all around them, and no one did anything to stop the abuse. So many were hurt, so many souls were damaged, and no one spoke up. Complicit silence was the mechanism that let the cruelty continue over and over again, while millions were hurt and damaged for life.

But now people see what went on, and we can change the future. They can help others heal and not repeat the sins of their fathers.

GOD SPEAKS TO ME AGAIN

Women must take the lead; women must heal My Earth of the hatred and cruelty. Love must prevail. Love, kindness and understanding must rule the world. No more hatred; no more power over others.

Love thy neighbor, as you love yourself. Be kind to all. Make others understand what should be. Show others how to be kind and things will change. Make the world a better place for you and me. You are the world; you are the Children of GOD. We are the ones to make the change that is so badly needed.

All of this cruelty has brought us to this point. My children are waking up to reality, which is not what they were told or thought it was. The more that wake up, the better. The awakening is here—the time is now.

It will be good for mankind to move forward. It is time for Truth to reign over the world.

Keep telling the Truth. Keep telling the Truth. No one can deny the truth, even if they tried to forget. In the end, there is only the truth. Free will has been both good and not good. Man must choose Truth, Real Truth, not the disturbed way of the past. Truth will set you free. So only the truth will do.

Make the world a better place for you and me. There will be help all around you. Watch and listen, and you will see who can help. They are all around you.

Make the children see the new world. Keep the children safe, for they are the hope of the future. It always starts today. A new dawn – a new day, every day. Love the children; give them confidence that will help them seek the truth. The world will be a better place for all to see.

Make this cycle of pain stop. Bless and release Dad's soul to GOD. Bless and release yourself from him; free yourself from him for all eternity. Do it for the little girl who was betrayed by him, who was not protected by anyone. Stop being alone. Walk in the truth for it will set you free. You will heal in every way possible. That little girl will break out of the bubble and be free from pain, free from guilt, free from him! Make it stop and be free. Open your heart to be free. It is time.

Your sister feels guilty that she could not protect herself or you; he was too strong. She was a little girl; he was too powerful. She could not protect you or herself. It was impossible for her, as a little girl, to stand up to him. She tried, but he tossed her aside, hurting her because he was just too strong. He pushed her to the ground, and she was frightened and sad that he had hurt her. How could he do that? You were so tiny, and he was so strong. She yelled "Stop! Stop!" but he lashed out and hit her again. Mom was devastated. She could not protect herself from his rage, and she could not protect any of you from him. It was everyone in survival, it was everyone for themselves, but you were just two tiny girls – it was what happened then, and now. You must heal those little girls.

There are two of you all grown up; no need to fear him anymore. Both of you can go to him and tell him you know the truth. There will be no way for him to deny what has happened. It is how it should be, two sisters on your journey to the truth; it will lead to the light for both of you. It is the only way to heal. He must know that you both know. There is no denying the truth with both of you right there. You have both talked to your Mom. You both know the real truth and he cannot deny it anymore. It is eating him alive, as it should.

I am so proud of you; this has been a long journey. You will not be tired any more, once you set yourself free of this burden.

Your sister will feel better too, the weights are lifting in your souls and the light will shine down on both of you. It will be like a revelation; peace will fill both of you. The time to cry over this is done. The light will shine through it will be over and done. You will both heal, and I will be with you and so it is. And, so, it is.

Remember to be patient with others; they are on their own journey. You may remember and process things faster or slower than another soul; however, you must let them travel their road to the truth. Be compassionate with others, as they progress in their own time and space, to move towards their truth, even if the two do not align. Even shared experiences are not always perceived exactly the same by both souls. Guilt, fear and denial are all very strong instincts and can enter the process of accepting and learning the truth, as you walk your path to the light. Learning to let go of the guilt and fear will eventually help overcome denial.

When there is such abuse, where young children are involved, and as we open ourselves to the truth, it can be painful and sad. We can progress through a full circle of emotions. Many times, we are transported back to the age of when the abuse happened, so you must protect those little children as they go through their awakening. They are very fragile and will undoubtedly go through another cycle of trauma as they progress through the process of healing one bubble at a time.

There are times when confronting the abusers can assist in the process. Just the fact that they must acknowledge what happened should be enough to validate your truth. It does not even matter what the response is or how it is acknowledged or denied. You will be able to see the truth through whatever response you receive. Even if they do not acknowledge openly to you, they will have to acknowledge it to themselves, what terrible things they have done. It is their reckoning; it has to be done. It must be done for it is written. "It must be done for the glory and power is mine."

Give yourselves time to heal. This revelation and acknowledgement of what happened takes time to process and heal. Be patient and kind to your inner child; they deserve to be loved, protected and understood. Help the inner child heal and grow. It will eventually give you peace that is a long time coming.

GOD CONTINUES…
MY WORLD IS A VIRTUAL PRISION

The world has become more and more like a prison, when a few elites rule the masses. The world was never supposed to be ruled by a few. Mankind was put on Earth to enjoy all that GOD gave them. All things the sun, the ocean, trees, deserts, mountains, forests and more were given to all My people. It was all put here for mankind to enjoy. No one is supposed to be or have anything more or less than the next. All of it is for all to enjoy. If love ruled the world, all would be able to partake in all of it.

There would be no elite people, no rulers. All would have everything; all would lack nothing.

When greed and ego rule the world, we have utter chaos. Everyone is trying to hurt each other. People are suffering and dying from lack, when there is no need for such a thing. I have given you a world where no one should suffer. It is at the hands of man himself that My people are suffering. You all pray for Me to end the hunger –end the suffering on Earth. But what man does not realize is that you suffer because of yourselves. Free will has led man to think he is superior to one another and superior to other creatures of the earth, superior to all sometimes, including GOD.

The Earth can sustain all my people if you stop the hatred for each other. Stop the wars. Stop trying to control the world. You think you know better than GOD.

They think they can save the world by killing most of the population and save only man's choice of who should live and who should not.

Man thinks that he will create a superior race; that if the world is divided into as many different factions as possible, or groups based on baseless division, that everyone will turn on each other and destroy all the different groups based on race, religion and other manmade categories.

I am sending you this message. "I WILL NOT STAND FOR THIS." Man will not enslave my souls for eternity – man thinks he can create life and destroy life as he chooses. Man thinks he can control how each of you thinks, eats, lives, moves and breathes. I will not have it!

What you now call medicine and medical care, is noteworthy to know is not health or care or a solution to illness or disease. Man has created all the disease and suffering by trying to make you believe they can help you with their medicine, most of which is poison. That is not how I envisioned you to live.

Man is so arrogant that he believes he knows better than GOD; that he can unlock the secrets to life. You have been told nothing but lies.

You have been made to believe that you must take all those medical treatments to get better.

I am telling you there is a better way. GOD's way! All of this has been very bad for mankind.

I have given you all you need to have abundance in life. There is an abundance of love, joy, happiness and yes, health. You do not need to continue destroying the earth with what you purport to be science and scientific advancements.

Each and every soul has the ability to heal itself. Each and every one of my children has the ability to heal the sins of their fathers and the ability to heal the sins of themselves and walk to the light. Come into the Truth; not manmade truths.

TRUTHS OR MANMADE LIES?

Until we are able to bring the masses to the understanding that GOD's Truth is definitely not man's made-up truths that they have been creating for centuries to keep you under their control and to keep you away from the real Truth of God.

Your teachings are wrong. Your teachers are corrupted by greed and ego; you have been fed a false reality. You have been fed so many lies and created so many rules and laws—all manmade laws. Manmade laws have not served My people well. Manmade laws have led us to where we are today! Embroiled in total chaos and hatred for one another, as well as a total disregard for life itself and the lives of one another is where you are. We must seek out the truth. We must move the masses to the light, we must evolve as a whole to stop the tyranny, stop the mutilation of our brothers and sisters.

We must stop the senseless experimentation; stop the slavery and medical tyranny. But, most of all, mankind fears the few who have aspirations to control your body, your minds and ulti-mately your soul.

I will not have it!

The Earth and mankind must act immediately to counter what is going on. Your world depends on it. Your world requires each and every one to embark on their journey to the light and to the Truth.

Mankind must reject all that is not true. Man must reject all that seems to be not right. If it feels like it is not right; it is not!

CRITICAL THINKING IS INDEPENDENT, BUT NEEDS TO BE COLLECTIVE

Let me explain, we must teach our children critical thinking, because if they learn again to question what is happening and what is being pushed on them from every direction, they will see the light breaking through the bubble, as well.

As we each begin breaking out of our bubbles chipping away at the false information that has been forced upon us, we will see it all!

We will break one bubble at a time, until we eventually see the light and truth before us with no doubt, no fear and know that it is the way.

All the technology and all the so-called science is just an illusion that has distracted My souls from their journeys. All the technology, all the experiments and all the cruel mutilation of My people, in the name of science and progress, is just an attempt to control and gain power over others.

All that is happening now that they want to call science, is creating the distraction of mankind. They say that you are too smart for your own good. Maybe that is so.

I say that you have overstepped your boundaries. You have eaten the fruit of the one tree that I have asked you not to.

Man has not advanced, but regressed to cause so much pain and suffering to others. It must stop. You still have not realized that you only need what I have given you. You do not need manmade cures. Your bodies are capable of many things. You must go back to nature and stop destroying your world. Stop changing your world with drugs and stop the manufacturing of drugs that create more problems than they solve. Your so-called health services are just managing your manmade symptoms from all the drugs you claim will help. They never seem to cure anything and never will. They just create more disease and pain. Stop, stop, stop!

You must convince My souls that they must take their journey. They must live in the truth, when they are able to journey to the truth.

Then, and only then, will mankind make the progress they need to be rid of this manmade hierarchy of sorts that has been destroying your world.

As the souls begin their journey, they will push harder and harder to seek their own Truths and will be compelled to stay on their journey to the Truth. It will be impossible to turn away from the Truth.

The yearning to continue will compel them to stay the course; to stay on the path to the light and Truth. It will be impossible to turn away from the Truth.

It is for each and every one to begin the journey. Those who refuse to come into the Truth will perish from this world. They will have served their purpose, which was to show the others the wrong path. The path that should never have been taken.

There is no room for doubt, for those who accept their journey will be chosen to walk into the light with the Lord.

There is no greater journey; no greater purpose in life than to seek the truth and follow the path to the light.

There is no other choice than to follow the path. Anything other than this will surely be the total destruction of mankind.

There is no time to waste; there is only the journey.

There are many who will begin leading the masses. It will not be they who are in your world, who think they have power and control. Those who think they are making the world a better place for them. Their reality is so distorted, they actually think that just a few people will control the world and the only ones who will have everything is them.

I TELL YOU, I WILL NOT HAVE IT!

All the elite people who have taken over and taken power from the people are not the arbiters of Truth. They are the arbiters of manmade laws and rules that are all contrary to My will for all.

They have continued to push untruth on all. They have destroyed your churches and your schools. They have created such a divisive environment in the hopes of separating and conquering all.

Unfortunately, many have followed them under the false pretense that unity can be created through labeling and division.

If they do not strike down these practices in every corner of My Earth, I will have to intervene. There are only two things the world needs, Love and Truth.

It does not need to be reframed or renamed, or announced in any other terms. LOVE and TRUTH! Yes, it is just that simple.

When will you all understand that man was not meant to divide and conquer. Every group of people, no matter how you choose to label them, has suffered throughout time. There is no one group that was spared suffering and pain. All races and religions have been exploited and killed. Look hard at history. Slave states were just poor people of all nationalities, of all races, of all religions, over the course of humankind.

The continued exploitation of man will go from one group to another as long as you try to label my children. The more labels, the more groups to exploit. Stop the labels. Stop the division.

Unify all mankind. All are just My souls, who must start their journey to the truth. In My world, the souls are all the same.

The souls are all My children. The souls are all heading back to Me. Bring My souls as one back to Me. No more labels; just Love and Truth.

Keep your eye on the ball and follow the path. Take the journey with all your brothers and sisters. Keep the faith always – keep the faith. Know that your path is yours alone to experience and to follow, but the result is always the same, Love, Light and Happiness in knowing the Truth.

RE-CREATION

Re-Creation is where our souls begin; they re-create the sins of past generations, and so the cycle goes. It is only when we seek the Truth that the generational traumas of the past are truly released to the universe and the real journey to creation begins.

The truth comes slowly at first so your human senses can process what has happened. There is so much to explore for each of you. It can be a lot to accept, and some will not want to accept what was. They will deny all that has happened, hoping to lock it away just a bit longer, but their yearning for the truth will be so overwhelming that when the truth unfolds it is just too difficult to deny. It will all just start to fit together, one small piece at a time. You may not see it at first, but as each new bit of information comes back to you, it will make more sense and you will understand and accept the truth.

You must all have faith, that what is being given to you is from Me. You will need to stop the doubt, stop the fear of knowing what is. When you stop doubting, the information will flow much more smoothly and you will be able to see how things were, much more clearly.

The sooner you seek the truth, the sooner you will heal and move the next generation to a higher level of understanding.

We must move mankind to a more evolved state of being, which can only be achieved by the continuous journey to Truth and Light.

It is so past time for mankind to put down the weapons of mass destruction and move to cohesive unity throughout the world.

We need a collective consciousness of souls to save the world from total destruction.

Man is not listening to Me. They are continuing to try to control everything in this world —people, resources, money, and ultimately power over everything.

Their collective consciousness is in the wrong place. There will be no evolution until the powers that be are dismantled – and it needs to happen simultaneously. There is no room for the tyrannical world leaders in your world to exist. They are keeping us from moving mankind to a higher level of consciousness. There is a massive shift that must take place for this to happen as it should.

I have put in motion many souls to unite for the good of all mankind. They will see the truth; they will accept their roles in bringing my souls to the awakening. It is already happening and will continue to happen until there is an indescribable wave of energy that comes over the awakened souls. Love and peace will be the most powerful forces that push Truth in the forefront of all that is.

BACK TO THE LITTLE GIRL IN THE BUBBLE

The little girl in the bubble is crouched down holding her legs close to her – all alone, feeling very alone.

No one pays attention. She is on her own. She is crying. Why did he do that on the bed? Then, when he locked the door in the bathroom? Why did he take my clothes off? Why did he take his off? He pushed my head down into his naked lap while sitting on the hamper. I could not get free. I cried, no one heard me. Mom was next door having tea with the neighbor. He always hurt me when Mom was next door. When he decided to let me go, I ran to my room crying. I just stayed on my bed in my room sobbing. I may have been 5 or 6 years old at the time. No other memory. He just did it when Mom could not see and went off laughing, telling me if I told on him he would beat me and hurt me. I was frightened – he was so much bigger and stronger than me. I was powerless to protect myself and he knew it.

First grade was difficult. Still wetting my bed. I tried to hide it un- til Dad was gone and then, do the laundry very quickly and make my bed as quickly as possible, so no one would know.

I became very sick that winter. I had a terrible time breathing. I could not breathe, and I could not eat. Coughing so hard I wet my pants. My chest felt like an elephant was sitting on it. I was home for a while, and it just kept getting worse and worse. Mom would pick me up out of bed and put a sheet, pillow and blanket on the couch for me to lay in the living room. I could barely lift my head off the pillow, I was so weak. I could not stop coughing. It hurt my chest to cough. My whole body was trembling with fever. After a week or so, and no school for me, the teacher decided to send homework for me to complete as best I could. At that time, I was supposed to be learning to read. It was just such a challenge for me to sit up for a few minutes that I was not able to concentrate on learning. I fell behind at school. Mom finally brought me to the doctor's office. I remembered the word he used was 'parapertussis.' I thought for sure I would not live. Maybe, that was what was supposed to happen. The doctor talked to Mom very softly for a few minutes. Then, he told me that I would need to take the medicine he was going to give Mom and rest as much as possible. I was contagious and had to be home for weeks until the fever was gone, and the coughing stopped.

It did not sound good to me and I just felt awful, so I did what he said. It certainly was not hard. I could barely move and all I wanted to do was sleep. Everyone at home stayed away from me. They would say "hello" from the other side of the room and go off to do their own thing.

The homework kept coming every day. Many times, I could not sit up long enough to complete my assignments. Mom tried to help me with my reading. It was very hard for me, since I really did not have a teacher. I was learning my alphabet and reading at the same time. Trying to write three-word sentences like, "See Jane run. See Spot jump."

Every day was the same. Mom would move me from my bed to the couch, where I would stay until my siblings got home from school. I just wanted to get better to be able to walk and run and play outside. I wanted to get better, to eat solid food without vomiting and go to the bathroom without Mom carrying me.

I was out of school for about a month and a half. I felt so isolated from everyone and everything.

When I finally was able to walk and breathe again, I was still very weak, like a ragdoll. I was so far behind in school. The other kids had learned so much while I was away. My teacher tried to spend extra time with me. My Mom had to go to the school to talk to the teacher. The teacher did not feel that I would be able to catch up. They felt that I would have to repeat first grade. I was really struggling.

I cried when she told me. I did not want to be dumb. Then, what would they do with me? I was terrified: I tried so hard, did so much work every day at home to catch up. They decided to transfer me to the slow class and promote me to second grade. I would be with the kids that needed extra help. I was not sure that would work; what if "my family" did not want me because I was not smart enough? It was devastating for me to go from the top class to the bottom class.

I read all the books they gave me for the summer. I read all the time and Mom helped me. She took extra reading and work-books from the school for the summer.

All I kept thinking was "I could not be anything less than perfect because they might get rid of me."

Eventually, when I went to the second grade in the fall, my new teacher realized very early on that I really did not belong in her class and spoke to Mom and the other teachers about moving me immediately up to the next class.

I was not really well; I had trouble breathing all the time. When I tried to breathe in deeply, I would get lightheaded, and my chest always felt like the air did not want to go in my lungs. When I tried to run fast or play outside, it was not uncommon for me to get dizzy and have to sit down.

Well, by fourth grade I was doing really well in school. I was back in the top class, and my grades were good. I loved my teacher. I was always doing extra work to keep ahead of the class. I never wanted to fall behind again. I guess, back then, you might have called me the teacher's pet. I ended that year so excited about school, and happy that I had such a wonderful teacher.

The next year, that same teacher advanced to fifth grade, and I had her again. I was beyond elated. Someone would take care of me. What a relief! I knew someone would help me stay ahead of my grade and be concerned about me. Then, shortly after the school year started, we found out that my teacher had to have surgery and would be out of school about 6 or 8 weeks. We would be having a substitute teacher. An older woman, who was doing her student teaching, would take over the class until she returned. I was devastated. What would happen now? Just a couple days after the new teacher came in, we were all doing our class work while the teacher was writing on the chalkboard with her back to the class, when the boys on the side of my desk decided to be funny and knock all my books off my desk on the floor to cause a scene. The books crashed to the floor. As the teacher turned around to ask what happened, the boys said I pushed my books to the floor. She never even asked me or gave me a chance to say what happened; she went into a rage like something snapped inside her and started yelling at me. I tried to tell her I did not do it, but she just got angrier. She began yelling at me for interrupting her class and never gave me a chance to speak. She started threatening me to tell my teacher when she returned how bad I was. How could she do that? Certainly, my real teacher knew me, she knew I was a good kid. There was no way she would believe this woman. She would know I was telling the truth, right?

My head was spinning. How did this all happen? But then again, she was just another adult who did not want to hear the truth. She was angry and mean. She said she would call my parents and tell them how I was taking advantage of her as a substitute teacher, and I would be sorry for lying.

That did not work out well for me. I was in big trouble, yet again, for something I did not do. Dad was Irate; I was punished and could not do anything or go anywhere until I had a good report back from the teacher. Mom sort of knew this lady. She was from our small town and there had been rumors that she was extremely strict and was not nice to her own children. I think she knew I was telling the truth and that the substitute teacher was trying to make a name for herself. Trying to show everyone that she was going to have control over her classroom, no matter what. Her poor behavior gave the boys in class a free pass to harass me and cause more trouble and continue to blame it on me. This teacher was so cruel to me. I could not say or do anything without her criticizing me. I was just plain miserable in school. Finally, my mother went to school to discuss this with her. My Mom realized she was just a hateful woman who had no business teaching school. Mom was pleasant and we got through the next couple months.

But it did not end. Before she left, she wrote a scathing letter to our regular teacher saying how terrible I was. She stated that I was a liar and how disrespectful that I had been. So, when my teacher came back, and told me how disappointed she was in me, it was devastating for me. I had loved that teacher and now, she hated me. I could never win her trust back. I did my work. I talked to no one – none of the girls wanted to play with me at recess, because everyone thought I would get them in trouble. I was so glad when that year ended and so was Mom.

I was just trying to survive one day at a time in my little bubble, crouched down, sobbing. No one stands up for me; no one loves me. I will survive; there is no other choice.

Sixth grade, OH MY GOD! That nasty cruel substitute teacher was given a full-time position permanently the next year, and you guessed it, I had her for my homeroom teacher and several classes. My mother requested they move me to another teacher and the school refused. They wanted me in the top class, because I was doing really well. I kept my head down, I did my work and only talked to her when necessary. She was always taunting me like a bully, as well as making a concerted effort, whenever possible, to turn the other teachers against me. She even tried to tell the other girls not to hang around with me at recess, because I was a troublemaker. I was just miserable all year.

Thankfully, some of the teachers that had been there for years were spending a lot of time observing her trying to figure out why she was so rigid. There had to be someone who saw through her cruelty. I was not sure what was going on until, one day, I actually heard her trying to say bad things about me to the other teachers in the hallway.

Shortly thereafter, my English teacher asked me to come to her class one day. She felt compelled to let me know she thought that I was a very smart and a very nice person. She explained she never likes to listen to what others have to say about someone. She always judges for herself how people treat her before she decides if someone is a good person. She emphasized that she felt I was a good person and for me to just try to do my work and not to be changed by people who did not have my best interest in mind. She told me how smart I was and how well I was doing. She encouraged me to keep working hard and told me I was really talented and do not let anyone take that from me. I was so grateful for that conversation, because when someone of authority or who has a title continuously beats you down, especially at such an impressionable age, it can stigmatize a child for life.

I had already locked myself in that bubble again since my encounter with that wicked teacher. Nice and tight, right along with all those other memories of others who had hurt me.

I was just trying to survive, one day at a time.

Mom was substituting when I was in 6th grade, at the same school I was in. I think she talked to some of the other teachers. She asked them to keep an eye on me and let her know if there was a problem. My mother saw for herself how cruel this lady acted, and not just to me. She was also harassing a couple of boys at the same time. It was undeniable when you saw her in action. That woman tried to push kids into doing things, just so she could 'discipline' them. None of the other teachers were warming up to her. She continued to try to provoke me and blame me for all sorts of things that had nothing to do with me for the entire year. She was truly an evil person who should never have been around children. She sent notes regularly to my Mom that year, trying to say all sorts of things about me, but my Mom had her number by that point. At least she was not telling my Dad what that woman was saying about me. Mom tried to protect me from Dad's wrath in that arena. I was so thankful for that.

I prayed to God to make her go away, that someone would fire her for the way she treated the kids; but it did not happen. She was evil, hateful, volatile and such an awful human being. I hated sitting behind her and her family in church on Sundays. I found myself feeling sorry for her two daughters. How much pain were they going through living with a woman who truly hates children? What a miserable life they must have with this cruel mother.

June could not come soon enough for the end of the school year. I would be free from her.

Mom graduated college and finished her student teaching in her late 40s. I was so excited for her. She took a full-time job in a neighboring small town. She would not teach in the same system as that wicked teacher. Her student teaching in my school and the ordeal with that wicked woman had surely been enough. Mom could not bear to see the cruelty that woman inflicted on the children and would not be around her.

Dad was so angry when she graduated, and no one could understand why. We were all so proud of her. She had two college friends, both older women with husbands and families like her.

Mom would sometimes drive to classes with them so they could use just one car to save money. When graduation was done the other husbands wanted to celebrate their wives' graduations with the three couples going to dinner. When Mom asked Dad to go, he was so angry that they had to go to the bedroom and close the door. All we heard was yelling and Mom crying. "It is just dinner to celebrate our graduation, can you just please come for me, please." She begged him and he just screamed louder, that her and her friends were trying to make him feel stupid because he never went to college.

Yes, and there you have it! He felt less than. So he would do nothing for her and her "uppity friends." He would not be around them. One more time, she tried to console him, appease him and calm him down, but of course he refused to go. My heart poured out to her. I asked Dad later why he would not do that for Mom, I did not understand. He told me to mind my own business. There was never any discussion after that. Of course, you never tried to argue with Dad; there was certainly no winning when he was mad. I dropped it.

Mom would take me with her, and I would help her decorate her room with some creative bulletin boards. I helped her clean and organize and inventory her books and supplies. She did not yell at me, we just worked together chatting and having a good time. I was so grateful for our time together. I began to have so much respect and admiration for this woman, who became my hero. Sometimes, I would go to the classroom next door and help her friend, who taught the same grade level. She was a lovely, kind person and I enjoyed helping her as well.

This was a special time for Mom and me to just be in a new environment, where she got to be in charge of her classroom, and she could help children to prepare for the world. Several years went by and one afternoon, I finally got enough courage to ask Mom if I was adopted. It took years for me to ask. Mom was perplexed, she was not sure where I got that from. She calmly explained that I was not adopted. She told me about being born in a blizzard and how Dad drove her to the hospital in a truck and dropped her off on his way to Boston to deliver a load of freight.

I could not believe after all that time that I was not adopted. Was Mom really telling the truth? She showed me my birth certificate with her name as mother and Dad's name as father and talked to me about looking like my siblings. She wanted to know why I thought that, so I explained the story my brothers had told me over and over until I believed it to be true. She never realized how much it hurt me until that moment. My whole life I thought if I was not perfect that they would get rid of me because I did not belong there. But maybe I did belong.

It is amazing how cruel children can be. Thinking that was a joke when it completely destroyed years of my childhood. I carried that burden by myself, along with all the abuse, until the day I gained enough courage to ask the question. It was a big step to confront the reality. I was more afraid of what the answer was than I realized – but at some point, I just had to know.

It always seemed that each time I needed someone to be on my side, someone to protect me, until this point, it never happened.

This entire experience reminded me how no one ever listened to me before. Why was the nasty teacher right? What made me wrong? How come no one believed me? Well, I just thought more of the same as it always was. No one listened, I was just a child; apparently adults are always right, end of discussion. I was a child, and I was not heard no matter what. Back in my bubble. I could just sit there crouched down holding my knees with my arms wrapped around them. Just alone. Just by myself. All by myself.

ANOTHER CHANGE AT HOME

Dad left his job and started his own business. It was at our house for some time, which was not a good experience for any of us. He was at home most of the time. Dad was answering phones, setting up the business and operating a trucking company, working with the drivers in and out of our home. Mom often was doing his typing. She was really proficient at typing; after all, she had worked in the office at the mill before she married Dad. Dad typed with two fingers and was much slower. Mom was expected to do whatever he needed; it was always what he needed first, even though she had a job teaching and took care of us and the house.

WHAT ABOUT HAVING FRIENDS?

All my friends at school were having sleepovers and overnight birthday parties. I was not allowed to go, because we could not reciprocate. I found it really hard to have friends when the other girls were spending so much time together and I was not allowed to participate. I was only allowed to see my friends at school.

I just did not understand why I could not have real friends – and no one really included me in anything after a while, because they knew that I could never go. The girls were all good friends and talked about all the fun they had when they were together for their sleepovers. The games, the late nights up talking and laughing. I was isolated from it all. They talked to me in school, but I never felt like I was part of their group of real friends.

So, I studied every night until the wee hours of the morning. I did not get in trouble. I got good grades, and I suffered in silence. This was a lesson that was learned at a very young age, and it was solidified throughout my life. Be quiet; do not discuss anything that went on at home. Do not cry. Be seen, but not heard – and never question an adult. What you think and feel does not matter – nobody cares. Just learn to cover up your pain and live with it.

I used to go to church every week. I walked about a mile, met a girlfriend on the way, and we went together. I used to pray to Jesus every week, but what could I tell him? No one could hear me. I prayed in silence, but I had to be careful, because I did not want him to be angry with me. What if I said something that would make him angry or told him something that happened at home? He might not believe it anyway. So, I just prayed the prayers I was taught in religion class and church. I was afraid to tell him anything else, he might not love me either – if he knew.

What would happen? Maybe he would not want to love me. Maybe he would say it was my fault. I knew it was not, but he might not believe me, because adults were always right, and I was just a kid. I wanted God and Jesus to love me. Please: some-one needs to love me. So, instead of talking to God, I just prayed the prayers they taught me over and over again. I went to con-fession. I would tell the priest that I was sorry for anything that happened during the week as if it was always my fault.

Go to school, study hard, get good grades, help Mom at home, help Mom at school, and stay out of Dad's way at home. Stay in your room. There you have it – and go to church every week. Be smart, be good and stay out of the way.

My siblings had jobs. Some worked on a local farm. I convinced my parents to let me work there, as well, one spring on the weekends and then all day during the summer. We got up very early, before dawn, and came home after dark most days. I thought, finally, if I could work, I would be able to save enough money to buy a new bike. I wanted a new bike all my life, since I was old enough to remember anything. My brothers had new bikes, but I could not have one. We could not afford to buy a bike for me. My brother, who was two years older than me, re-ceived a new bike for his birthday one year. It was a sparkly rust color with a banana seat. He would ride the bike to baseball practice and games. I would beg him to go with him. So, he let me run alongside him on his bike to the baseball field. I was only allowed to ride the bike if he was not riding it. Well, he lived on that bike, so I was never allowed to use it, I just walked and ran alongside him as he rode to baseball practice and games.

I remember the neighbor's oldest daughter had an old bike that she used when she was young in her garage. She was about 13 or 14 years older than me. She did not ride her bike anymore and so, one day when she saw me watching my brother riding, she came over and asked if I wanted her bike and she gave it to me for my sister and I to ride. Even though my sister was four years older than me, she did not know how to ride a bike. She never had one either. The bike was old fashioned and kind of rusty, but I was thrilled to have it. I brought the bike home and washed and polished it. I would share the bike with my sister. My sister never rode the bike. I did not understand why she did not want to ride it, but later in life found out she just did not know how.

It was always about the boys. The girls just did not matter. They were supposed to clean the house, cook, iron, learn to sew and stay thin. Yes, stay thin; do not build up muscle, because that would not be feminine. That seemed like it was extremely important: stay thin and be feminine. My sister and I were taking prescription diet pills in grammar school and high school. We could not gain weight. We had to be extremely thin like our mother, who weighed all of 100 pounds soaking wet even after having six children.

In high school, I wanted to try out for cheerleading. There were no girls' sports at that time. My father was furious and did not want me to get muscular legs, so I had to quit tryouts.

I was elected freshman class president. I spoke to the teachers and the student council, and I was amazed that people were interested in what I had to say. I did not feel like I was saying anything overly profound, but I seemed to be able to get people to come together and work toward some common goals. Some interests for our freshman students were actually addressed, to my amazement.

RE-CREATION OF THE PAST

What was, and what happened, in the past is very important in the journey to healing. Remembering or reconstructing what happened previously will help us to avoid the same patterns in the future. Once the soul has seen the mistakes of the past and recognizes them, it is so much easier to avoid them in the present.

Healing cannot begin until we acknowledge what has happened in our past. Seeing past generations and acknowledging those events will give us a greater understanding and perspective. This knowledge can give us a guide to what shapes our human behaviors and responses in the present.

We can always look back to previous generations as it will show us the evolution of our ancestor's journey. Although each soul will have its own journey. The journey of those who came before us will help us understand why we are where we are.

Generational trauma is part of our make-up. It is, as they say, part of our DNA; part of who we really are. Trauma is passed down through one generation to another, not consciously, but passed down nevertheless. Everyone learns from their parents, and models their behavior and responses to outside stimulus on how their parents responded to certain situations.

For example, if your mother was physically abused, made to feel less than, or made to feel nothing – she was of no interest or importance – then that is what her truth becomes, which is also what she projects to her children. When someone is not allowed to contribute to a conversation, or able to have an opinion, it greatly impacts the experiences they allow themselves to have. When there was no give and take as a child, no acknowledgement of value added by a child, it becomes so difficult. A child will struggle as an adult to feel heard; to feel relevant to themselves or others. Relationships are so difficult due to diminished self-worth, that one can have an inferiority complex about almost anything. Each relationship one enters as an adult may be entered into as feeling less than others. I cannot stress that enough: it is just so important for each individual person to be acknowledged and be heard at every age and stage of their lives.

GRANDPARENTS: THE STORY

GRANDPARENTS: THE STORY

The Story of Grandma and Grandpa is a perfect example of the crushing of a soul. This was such a poor soul, who was not acknowledged or heard. Grandpa had a very overbearing personality, even as a young man. He never allowed Grandma to develop and grow in their relationship or individually. Many will say "that is the way it was for women in the early 1900s," trying to make it look like it was normal to have a husband who was overbearing and just dismissed his wife's opinions. Grandpa was always right, after all; she was just a child (10 years younger than him). Many women had been brushed aside; in fact, for generations women with great ideas have been dismissed as less than, made to feel that their ideas were not important.

Let's look at her story:

Grandma was born in 1896. As a small girl, her parents separated and her dad left. He moved about 10 miles away, just far enough that she never saw him as a young girl. He just disappeared from her life. Her mother struggled to work and support them. One day, her mother – my great-grandmother – met Grandpa at work. He was looking for a wife. When he met Grandma, he had to have her. She was 10 years younger than him, but it did not matter to him, he wanted to marry her.

Let's look at his story:

Grandpa was born in Boston in 1886, and was the oldest of four children. His parents immigrated from Canada to Boston. He liked to watch the boats in Boston Harbor as a young boy. He went to school until 6th grade. His parents came to Connecticut. He began working at a textile company and moved up to become an electrical engineer. His younger brother went into the service. His sisters married well, to very intelligent men, as was the custom in those days, men who would take care of them.

GOD UNRAVELS A LITTLE TRUTH

I am here to tell you that no soul, not one, has ever been above another. No one is wiser than another just because they were physically stronger. Physical might does not make someone a better decision maker or superior.

This is where mankind has gone wrong! Men thought for centuries they were superior and that they should rule over women and weaker men. It is all ego. It is this superiority, ego, control and power that has led to the dilemmas of today.

Free will has been a blessing and a curse. I must tell you again. No soul is superior to another. You are all tied together, and when one soul hurts another – when one soul takes advantage of another – they hurt the collective souls of all, including themselves.

This is worth thinking about; as you control or hurt others, you hurt yourself.

For generations men felt superior and had to be in control, be tough, not cry, and not be weak. So, came the superiority they thought they owned their wives and yes, their children, as well. More like possessions, they had the right to abuse their wives and keep them from doing anything they wanted. They kept their wives locked up and unable to develop their own unique talents and gifts.

Women were here to serve men, have babies, stay home, care for the house and children, and anything that their husbands wanted. Men were shown by their fathers to disrespect their wives and beat their children for generations. Manmade rules supported this, as did manmade religious beliefs. Women lived in virtual prisons for generations. They were shown how to be submissive, like their mothers, just to keep the peace. After all, men were drinking heavily in those days and women did what their husbands commanded. They did what they were told. After all, men took care of their wives and they provided for the family, so they were entitled. If women did not do as they were told, then there were consequences.

Unfortunately, no one realized that two people in a relationship both had the GOD-given right to be equal partners and to be able to work together so both partners were able to reach their full potential. No soul was supposed to beat the other into submission. No one was supposed to Lord over another or look down at them as less than themselves.

How did this come about that men felt so superior that they had the right to beat and abuse their partners and children and thought it was a GOD-given right to treat their families like servants to make them feel important?

Mankind's teachers and leaders, both religious and social, have let generations of people suffer for no reason. The elders and the church leaders watched this evolve for centuries and did nothing to stop it. All of mankind's leaders have failed you. I will say it over and over again: your teachers and leaders have ALL failed you for generations. Many of your souls have recognized the abuse for generations; however, there have been so few who are willing to acknowledge the abuse and fewer have done anything to stop it.

When there were attempts to bring the abuse to light, to show the world this was real, their souls were persecuted and dismissed by others, who wanted to keep control.

The history of mankind shows, repeatedly, that man thinks those who want freedom and equality must be silenced by power, ego and might. Wars that killed millions of souls have been fought by those who are all just looking for power and when anyone gets in the way they must pay. I am here to tell you, again, as I have for many centuries: no one is superior.

There are souls that I have chosen to deliver My messages, I have chosen many to deliver My messages over the years. You have not listened.

You are reading this book for a reason: it is to awaken the soul of mankind, and it starts with one soul at a time.

Please read through this book and understand that you must all journey together to change and save your world. It is so important that you start your journey!

Remember to bring others on the journey with you. If each of you brings another soul, then the world will begin to change quickly. Bring others with you on the journey and you will form GOD's army all over again.

Your soul must learn to question, to use your ability to decipher what is good and what is not. I am telling you that you can tell when something is not right. Listen to that voice inside of you. Your soul knows when something is not right. Listen to that voice inside of you! Your leaders have led, and continue to lead, you in the wrong direction. What they have done to mankind for power and might has been destroying your world. The destruction has been immense. It must stop. Look at what is happening to your world. What you call natural disasters are miniscule, compared to the destruction that man has caused on Earth.

I will tell you again, I have given you all that you need, there is plenty for all.

In a quest for more power and control, man has continuously tried to do anything in his power to retain control over all that is.

The few people that try to control will never be satisfied until they control it all.

Each of you must stand up to them and say no. You must not follow these leaders, who lead mankind down the wrong path. They have led all mankind down the wrong path – the path of self-destruction.

Mankind has created all the diseases. Yes, the disease that you now encounter is all created by all your scientists and your elite leaders. All the drugs, medicine and pharmaceuticals are just poison to mankind and poison to My Earth. Your free will has led you to sinister beliefs. They have continued to have devastating effects on My people and My Earth.

Experimentation, mutilation, murder, and human trafficking have all become so commonplace. The desensitizing of your children, the social control of your children's minds must all stop.

The time is now to stop what is going on in your world. Stop looking for a pill to cure the world. Look inside your soul. Start your journey. You already have all the ability that you need. You must start the journey, seek out your Truth, accept your Truth, move, and take your next step. Walk the path to the light. It is the only way for your soul and for all souls to journey to the light.

MASTERING MEDITATION

Meditating is one of the best ways to get in touch with your inner self and begin your journey to your truth It can be difficult, at first, to calm your mind and concentrate. Keep your mind relaxed and clear, it is the key to successful meditation. You must tune out all that is going on around you. Do not listen to the TV, radio, phone or any conversations going on in other rooms. Find a completely quiet place, where no one can interrupt. Close the door and tell others to leave you by yourself and please do not interrupt. You need quiet time to think and meditate with zero interruptions when you first start.

Once in a safe space with no distractions, the most difficult part is to clear your thoughts and just be still with yourself. Close your eyes and begin to breathe in through your nose and out through your mouth very slowly. Continue breathing and if some thought enters your mind like "I need to empty the dishwasher or the garbage," et cetera, stop yourself and say, "Not now, I will deal with that later." Go back to concentrating on your breathing: breathe in and exhale, keeping your thoughts at bay. Do not let them enter your head. Patience with yourself and practice are crucial. Always be patient with yourself: this is all part of the process, be patient like you would with a small child trying something new for the first time. Patience is a virtue I cannot express profoundly enough. Many of us need a lesson in patience, and here is a good place to learn that.

When you first start, you may find yourself overly aware of your surroundings. You may hear every noise around you, no matter how slight that noise is. It may seem amplified in the environment that you have created for your meditation, but try not to allow it to distract you from your mission.

Sometimes the slightest noise takes over and you seem to be drawn away from your meditation. You may think that you have lost your ability to concentrate. When that happens, immediately draw your attention back and focus on clearing your mind. Continue to breathe in through your nose and out through your mouth. Remember, if you get distracted anytime during the meditation, the process is the same: push that thought out of your mind and bring your focus back to your breathing. This is a great task to master. It is the beginning of showing you how to take over your mind and body, and teach them to relax cohesively. This is a huge accomplishment. Once achieved, you will be able to take the next step. Do not rush this process; it is extremely important. Do not be concerned that it is not happening on your time frame. In time, space and energy, there is no time as you experience as a human, there just is.

So here is where you start. This is the first step. You must practice quieting your mind and just be in the moment with nothing, no one, nobody—just be and stay in that moment for as long as you can. If a distraction comes in, release it to the void, release it to space and energy, and bring your focus back to quiet, clear nothingness. Again, sit with yourself and know this may be the hardest thing to do when you first start, but it will become easier and easier as you practice. Always, be patient with yourself this is a very big accomplishment for you.

Some of you will get this within a few sessions. For others, it may take weeks or even months. But remember, there is no timeline; there is only moving along the path knowing there will be success, if you truly continue to put in the effort. The more you concentrate and clear your mind the closer you come to that fully meditative state, where things will start to come to light, you will be moving on your path.

So, let us try again. Sit in a quiet space with no distractions around you.

Even when you are in a quiet space, when you start to close your eyes and begin to breathe with intention, you may feel like you are doing well, and some random thought enters your mind. That is perfectly normal, but you must tell yourself to forget that thought, center and focus on your breathing again and again until your mind is clear. Your mind will be void of all distractions and thoughts and will eventually give into your higher self. Sit quietly and breathe: concentrate on your breathing, inhale a little deeper each time and you will eventually have no choice but to clear your mind.

Again, I cannot stress enough how extremely important it is not to give up. Do not say 'I cannot do it,' or 'it does not work for me.' It works for all. Stay the course and keep doing this multiple times a day, if necessary. Clear your mind and breathe. Inhale through your nose, filling your lungs a little more each time, and exhale through your mouth slowly.

As a side note, it took me months to actually quiet my mind. I struggled with distractions from the physical space around me and then, when I mastered how to block those out, then my mind was constantly at war with itself. Random thoughts of things that happened at work or with family that bothered me. Many things entered my mind; things that happened with a friend and then, things from my past. Each and every thought brought me frustration and I did not understand why I could not concentrate on just plain nothing. Why is it so difficult to clear the mind? The more stress you have in your life, the more people who are in your life, the more that your experiences will continue to give you more random thoughts as you try to clear your mind.

This can all be part of the process. If you are not truly listening and ready to follow the path, it may take a little more evolution to teach you the patience necessary to let go of the control you think you have over everything in your life. This is a massive revelation for many, that they do not control all that is in their lives.

Many will not want to surrender their perceived control over their lives and the lives of those around them. Sometimes arrogance gets in our way, and we need to admit this and release that thought to the universe as well. What a concept.

Eventually, it will happen if you stay with it. You will have a clear mind with your eyes closed and it will be a blank space. It will be dark all around you and extend to infinity. You will know when you are there and then the truth will begin. Yes, it will begin when you reach the vast open space in the universe that just is.

I tried many meditations from many well-known individuals. I was always very careful to stay with positive meditations. Stay away from dark meditations that may lead you down the wrong path; remember you always have free will, which will allow you to deviate from your intended path, if you choose. But you can and will ask for guidance, and will receive it, if you are open to it. Just remember if it does not feel right, it is not right. We all know when something does not seem right for us.

PAY ATTENTION, AS YOU ARE THE AUTHOR OF YOUR JOURNEY!

You must make the choice to stay in the light. It is always a choice. Choose wisely.

Do not be discouraged; keep your focus on the future and how your journey will lead you down the path to the Truth and Light.

I practiced meditating whenever I had 10 to 15 minutes throughout my day. Sometimes, I would practice in my car or my office when others were not around. The more you practice, the more it becomes second nature. I was able to slow my breathing, lower my blood pressure and then, meditate longer. I reached the point where I could meditate for 20 to 30 minutes and thought, "How great is that?" I began meditating laying down or sitting in a chair and over time, I was able to mediate for longer and longer periods of time. Once you master the art of meditation, you will not need guided meditation. You may eventually be able to talk yourself through the meditations.

You will begin to feel a sense of calm and peace come over yourself. As you gain confidence, you will see just how powerful meditation is.

Learning to quiet your mind is one of the most powerful things you can do. Once you are in a deep meditation, the possibilities are endless. You can start by trying to make your body weightless and just picture yourself floating in the darkness; the endless space of infinity.

Meditation will change your life for the better. There is no doubt about it. The more proficient you become with relaxing your body and quieting your mind, the more you will be able to do.

MINDFULNESS EXPLAINED BY GOD

Once you have mastered the ability to clear your mind and just sit quietly with yourself, as well as master the true art of meditation, then I want you all to learn about mindfulness. Mindfulness is a state of being, where you will begin to open your mind to pure thoughts of Truth. The intention of seeing and accepting the Truth from GOD, which is sent to you through My methods of communication. I can communicate with you through many different ways. Sometimes it is most recognizable through meditation, which will lead to mindfulness.

You must focus with pure intention. What I mean is, do not try to control what thoughts come to you. You must just accept the thoughts sent to you. In other words, you will be quiet, your mind will be clear, and He will open your pathways to another dimension of communication. This will take practice. You must continue to do this over and over again.

All good things take time and effort, none of this is about immediate gratification. One must have faith and a true yearning to have a relationship with GOD. It must be mindful and sincere.

True faith in GOD will bring these changes about for you. True faith with no doubt and no fear, of what will be, when you are guided along this journey.

Do not try to control or lead the way; surrender to the Truth. Know that this is Him leading you where you need to go. "Know that I am with you on the journey. Know that I will not leave you. Have Faith in all that can and will be. There will be signs along the way, but you need to be open to them. They will be all around you."

Just as the darkness is all around you when you meditate, know that I am all around you every day and that you will have signs if you pay attention.

You will all have angels and guides to assist you; you will never be alone. Once you start your journey, we will all be there to assist you in staying on your individual path to the Truth.

You will start everyday with pure intention and slowly your mind will open up to the pure intention to follow My path. It is just waiting for you to start your journey. I have been waiting for all of you to start on your journeys. This is why you are here reading this book, right now.

It is time for you to start. The time is now for you to begin your journey. I have led you here. Now, here comes that free will thing again. Will you listen to Me calling you? Will you begin your journey today? Will you start your soul's journey to the Truth and the Light?

I have told many that the journey may be difficult at times. There is no easy way, but I am showing you the way. You must look and see, this is the way for all souls to journey to the light.

Start with the quiet spot, begin practicing your abilities to meditate. Begin to ask others to try. Spend time by yourself in a quiet state and clear your mind, VOID of all thoughts. VOID of all noise from around you. Just calm your mind. When your mind is quiet, then and only then, can the journey begin.

Some may see this calm come over you quite quickly; however, it will still take time to practice bringing yourself into the state where you seem to be no one – just nothing in the dark quiet, peaceful state.

Many great teachers of GOD have meditations where they tell you, you must let go of everything: your name, your identity as a human, your body. You must not identify with anything of this world. Just be still, be quiet, clear your mind and become pure in thought. Clear in thought that you are energy in the universe that is vast and goes on to infinity. You are part of a magnificent, endless universe that goes beyond your imagination. You are one with it all. You are part of everything beyond your ability to comprehend. You are one with all of it!

This is where you will be able to communicate with all of creation, with all of what is, all of what will be and with all possibilities.

So, let us get moving, let us get My souls on their journey. We must get going now. I cannot tell you how urgent it is to move all of you to the path, as quickly as possible.

It must happen; it cannot wait. We must evolve at warp speed to move mankind to save your souls.

GOD SPEAKS ON APPROCHING EVERYTHING WITH PURE INTENTIONS

As you experience the clearing of your thoughts through meditation, continue to meditate. Some may need to continue with guided meditations for a period of time. As a reminder, there is no time in space and energy; all just is, so do not try to put a timeline on your progress. Each soul evolves at their own pace, so just believe that you are where you are intended and supposed to be in the process at all times. You each need to progress at a different speed as your journey is unique to you. There are reasons that you will see things at a certain time. You must trust GOD to move you on your path at the right time; for you to do anything different would not serve you as an individual.

Some of you will need more proof or more reinforcement to take the next step on your path. Each step must be taken with no doubt and no fear. You must truly understand your own Truth with pure conviction —with pure thought that this is real and that this is the way. The only way, that there is one clear path, and you must know in your heart and soul that this is the way!

When you doubt the Truth you are being shown, I will go back and show you more examples of why it is so. Others may confirm it for you, and you may still doubt the Truth. You might be in denial, at times, so it may take longer for you to come to the Truth. Some people can grasp the Truth after being shown once or twice; for others, it may take many different ways to confirm that what you already know in your heart and soul is true.

Let me put that another way. Yes, you already know these things are true in your heart and soul, but as a human you have chosen to keep the Truth locked away in a box with a huge lock that no one can open. You hide the box and pray no one will find it. You leave it locked away in your subconscious, because it is just too painful or too unimaginable to believe or expose to others.

Yes, you all do it; not consciously, but you do it.

This is why your journey is so important. Your life and your soul's life depend on your ability to take your journey to the Truth, to walk the path that is here for you right now. Take the steps necessary to walk your path. Move through your journey. Do it with conviction that you will proceed with pure intention on your way to the Truth, even if it is painful at times – and it will be. Have faith and believe in Me. I am here. I am with you. I am the truth, and the light, and the way. The only way!

Remember, there are millions and millions of souls yearning to walk with you to the Truth and the Light, and back to GOD to be as one – as it should be. You will not journey alone. I will send other souls to cross your path, so you will know that you are not alone on your journey.

There will be millions on their journey at the same time. Help lead others to the start of their journey. The world will begin to awaken at a momentous speed to bring about the most profound shift that humankind will ever have experienced since the beginning of time.

Each one of you must take this as a calling to help each other – to help all. It is the way. It must happen. Just spread My message. Show others; lead them to the path. Lead them to the beginning of their journey. I will help them all.

I am going to tell you that this must happen. You must stay with it – stick to the course. Do not waver. Know that this is what must happen; this is your destiny, you must prevail. It will take time and you must stick with it. Perseverance is very important, so do not lose Faith when it takes a little longer for you or others. Encourage them to stay the course. Tell them to keep trying, it will come to them if they have unconditional faith – in Me, GOD.

Unconditional faith will lead you to Me!

Keep trying; keep the Faith. Meditate, Meditate, Meditate, until you reach nothingness – clear pathways.

Then, let the True Journey Begin!

It must be so. It must be so.

THE PATH IS YOUR JOURNEY ONLY YOU CAN WALK YOUR PATH

The little girl who hid that box of awful things from the past, that horrible TRUTH, so no one could find it: she did not have to accept it or process it if it was hidden away.

It all begins with the guilt and shame you feel as a child for what others have done to you, not knowing that it isn't your fault. A child does not have the capacity or knowledge to process that cruelty; the taking of a child's innocence is never their fault. Children have not yet developed the ability to communicate what is happening, and can't understand that these things are happening to them. A child who does not have the capability to protect themselves from those who are older or bigger than they are is also unable to help themselves.

 Adults who are mentally and physically superior in body and mind are able to prey on a child's innocence. Young children cannot understand why someone who is supposed to care for them and love them is inflicting pain and doing things that have to be hidden from others. Somehow it seems shameful or wrong. How could they possibly create such a painful experience? A child who has been abused looks inward – and seems, more often than not, to blame themselves. They will not typically put the blame where it truly belongs. They would never say what happened, as they were threatened that if they told anyone they would be in danger from that person again. The ability to process is overridden by fear.

Repression of their feelings is a learned response that comes from the feeling of powerlessness. So, hiding the bad experience seems like the only coping mechanism available at that time in the development of their small world. Sometimes it is the only way for them to survive the ordeals that just keep reoccurring. If a child were not able to repress the feeling of fear, guilt, shame, and helplessness, they might not make it to adulthood. Some do not make it through: they turn to alcohol, drugs or suicide, which can feel like the only options in their minds to make it all go away.

Children who suppress and deny the existence of the cruelty and torture they have had to endure will lock the memories deep in the box, placing them where no one will find them. No one will know the truth, no one can acknowledge what happened – not even to themselves. It may in fact be their only means of coping, the only way they can survive the incomprehensible actions of the past. Those deep dark secrets within them are just stuck inside. A child does not know who to trust, especially if someone who makes believe they love them and is supposed to protect them could do this. Is there anyone who would not hurt them if they were given the chance?

When they are with others who are supposed to love them, will they also hurt them? Many children learn not to trust adults for these very reasons. Many learn to stay away, keep to themselves, do not say anything for fear someone may hurt you. Just lock it away. Make the fear, shame and guilt be hidden from the world, lock it away, bury it in the deepest part of your mind, and never let it surface. Deny your truth and maybe you can forget for now – maybe, just maybe, no one will ever know. Until the day you cannot hide it anymore. Until that day!

KNOWING AND ACKNOWLEDGING

Deep seated memories locked away in the box can only stay there for so long. Eventually, when it is time, your journey must begin.

Denial is a very powerful human emotion. Many souls live in denial for years – maybe for lifetimes. Each soul will be drawn to take the journey, and eventually the time will come for each of us to step on the path. The goal here is to take the first step, from where you are right now. You will be drawn to it, and you will not be able to deny the gravitation for your soul to begin. Take the first step – and no matter what, you must follow your journey. Know that you are not alone. Know that GOD is always by your side. Your journey will be yours and yours alone; it will be your unique journey to your truth.

The acceptance of your reality is so important. All of what was, may take time to process. Your full range of emotions will all be part of the acknowledgement and acceptance of your TRUTH.

There is no journey that will be exactly the same – so each soul will experience different emotions at different times. There are times when these emotions may seem overwhelming, but the truth is, you did not cause or create what happened. These things happened to you and sometimes your reactions may not fit into your society's definition of a good reaction or acceptable response. Your experiences may have caused you to do what may have been inconceivable in certain circumstances. No matter what happened and regardless of your perceived part in it, remember you must face and acknowledge what was and continue to walk through the pain – and yes possibly the guilt – of reality. You must continue on the path. As you process and accept the truth of what was, you may need to sit in the moment for some time to process in your human mind, what was. But eventually it will be behind you, and you will move through it. Be patient with yourself as you face these truths: it is not easy to move from denial to acknowledgement and eventually acceptance. You must sit in your truth in order to move past it. Yes, let me say that again. You must sit in your truth in order to move past it. You may become sad, very sad at times for what happened to that little person, or for what you may have done to others. Be kind to yourself, and remember to love yourself through the process.

In order to process, you will go through several stages of grief. You may have conflicting thoughts about what happened, including fear, guilt, anguish, stress – and yes, anger – for those who may have put you in situations that caused so much pain for yourself and others.

Your human brain will have a hard time processing some events, but trust that you will eventually move past it. You will come out the other side of each locked up memory. You will journey though it and emerge with a clarity and deeper understanding of what was.

You must allow yourself to process all that was; without this step, the journey cannot continue. Process: feel the pain, the sorrow, the guilt and sadness. Cry when you need to, then walk through the experience and keep walking.

THE EMOTIONS

DENIAL

Denial, not acknowledging what was. What if someone finds out? Fear of what others may think of you: will they blame you, shame you, question whether this is your truth? Yes – all of that and more. It is very real and an extremely difficult step in your journey. Denial is what holds us in the same place. Denial stops us all from moving forward. Denial can be a very difficult feeling to overcome. If you take your journey you will move beyond denial and at some point, see what the Truth has to show you.

FEAR

Fear can immobilize the strongest of souls. It will stop you in your tracks, so to say. Fear of disappointing those you love, care for, and interact with. Those who will not understand or may continually criticize you can create an overwhelming fear. Fear of the unknown can stifle a soul and push you into very deep, dark places. Fear can cripple souls for many generations.

You must reach deep in your soul and know that this is the journey you cannot refuse to take any longer.

This is the journey you are meant to take – this is the only journey – you must stay on the path. You must stay on the path – and you must make the decision to walk with GOD. There is no other choice. The cycle will continue for generations unless you step on the path. Put the fear where it belongs – in the past – and take the step.

GUILT

Guilt is another all-consuming human emotion. It will weave in and out of your path. The fear of the first step is like jumping off a diving board into the pool for the first time: once you let yourself go and take the leap, you know you're going to be fine. Fear of the unknown is a normal human response to anything unfamiliar. Then comes the guilt, but once you're on the path be patient with yourself; practice self-love and acceptance so that when you feel that guilt surfacing you are able to tell yourself that all is okay, and you will no longer accept the guilt for what happened.

You must accept that you did not choose the circumstances or events to that happened to you. Realize that if you were a child, you were not able to help yourself or protect others from harm at that point in your life. There is no way a child can be responsible for the behavior of others.

Know that children do not have the capacity for cruelty or hatred or the ability to inflict pain and suffering on another. They learn those behaviors from others; this is something that they are taught by the actions of their abusers.

A child is born with a pure soul, in concert with all that is. It is the influence of others that damages them. It is that which we must seek to acknowledge, accept in our lives and in our soul that will set us free from all the burdens that life has created and put upon our souls. We must journey through these things and move beyond the guilt; this will give us the strength to continue on the path. Acknowledge, feel the feelings, and allow yourself to process. Do not try to move through too quickly; you will pass through the good and bad truths of your past.

All that we survive makes us who we are, how we think and how we act and react to all that will come. What we call character is all developed from our past experiences. It comes from knowing inside that we did not create the circumstances that we have so tidily packed away – but acknowledging that these were put in our path for a reason. This should help you see that life can be an obstacle course; it is there for you to get through. No one gets through unscathed. We are all affected by what we have been through. The test is to see if you can choose the path of light no matter what is thrown at you. Life is full of choices that each of us has to make every day. Travel the course every day, move along the path, choose wisely from this day forward, and continue on the path.

ANGUISH

Anguish can also throw us off course. We tend to want to stop when the truth of what was is too painful. Your free will is telling you, 'Just do not go there.' Try another solution: stay the course. Stay on the path to the truth. You may from time to time feel incapable of facing the things that happened, but once you see them and put them in proper perspective the agony will subside and you will be able to continue.

Know that you do not have to like what happened. In fact, you may hate what happened, but the purpose is just to acknowledge it, walk through it, and leave it in the past. There are millions of souls who are walking the path; they will help you along the way. When you need encouragement, someone will cross your path to help you through. You are never alone. When you need to sit with yourself, you must do so. It is a process, and I cannot repeat it enough. It is your journey and only you can take it.

ANGER

Anger can be all-consuming. At times you will definitely feel anger. Some say that anger can blind you; do not allow that to happen. Anger is an extremely strong human emotion and one that must be dealt with.

Meditation is a very powerful tool when it comes to dealing with powerful emotions such as anger. You must concentrate on why you are feeling such anger; remember, this feeling is part of the process. It is okay to feel anger. The unknown can create anxiety and anger all at the same time, so remember give yourself time for the healing process. The only thing you need to decide is how you will rid yourself of the anger. Understand that fear and anger are interrelated. Fear of the things that are both known and unknown can overwhelm the human response. Part of the process is finding a coping mechanism that works for you to bless and release these emotions – whether it be toward a certain set of circumstances or another person. Concentrating on the circumstances of what happened or what was done around you or to you, then thinking of the characters that were involved in the event, will help set the stage. Begin to look at it like it is a movie playing in your head; this will help you separate yourself from the event and look at it differently. It will help remove your fear of actually participating in the event itself.

Try looking at things as if you were someone else, like an outsider looking in. When you are watching the movie, you will gain a different perspective and allow yourself to process what happened without reliving the event as the main character. You can view it with empathy and love for the person who was hurt, and feel sorry or bad for them. It will give you the ability to feel the emotions of fear and sorrow for another person – the person who was you, at that time. Then you will need to forgive the perpetrator, so you may eventually forgive yourself.

You are not forgiving the person for their sake but for your own – you must release the fear, the guilt and blame that you have aimed toward yourself. This in no way will excuse the bad behavior of others but will release your own feelings of remorse and guilt about the event. You will now see after this that it was not your fault at all.

Remember that deep down inside, you have buried these events out of fear and misplaced guilt – and the only way to release it is to acknowledge it and recognize where the blame should truly rest.

Now that you are older you no longer have to look at the world through the eyes of a child's innocence and lack of knowledge of how powerful you really are. You are now capable of looking at the world from a different perspective, and you have the ability to decipher what was with a clearer understanding of things.

Looking through a clearer lens is like getting a new pair of glasses: things suddenly start looking clearer and clearer. This will give you the ability to move through all the emotions you were unable to process as a child and you will gain the strength to release the fear, guilt and anger that you have held inside for so long. Then you will begin to move on to the forgiving that needs to take place to move your soul to the light and freedom that GOD intended for all souls.

For your soul to be truly free it must disconnect from those who have hurt and damaged you in the human realm.

Each of us must find a way to release those who have caused us dis-ease in our lives. Each and every one who has hurt and damaged our trust – those who have kept us from the light – those who would keep us from our truth, our path, and our calling on this Earth.

In order to move forward, we must forgive and move on our path. Leave all that behind us and move on our journey.

Taking small steps on this part of your journey will ensure that you can keep moving forward. Take each event, then play the movie in your head during your meditation. See the perpetrators of cruelty, pain and injustice in the circumstances that surrounded these events. View it from the outside, feel all the emotions – do not suppress or push it off —feel the emotions.

See the perpetrator and know that they could not have acted as they did unless they were taught this behavior by others. They most likely had been abused as you were by someone in their past. Try not to judge them. Just observe and process. Now, try to imagine how they could have been shown or taught or been exposed to such cruelty in order to exhibit this type of behavior towards others. When you can actually see and feel the pain that they also had to endure, then you will see a clearer picture of the generational abuse and trauma all have experienced.

This is what we have been talking about in this book. Now at this point you may be able to bless and release these individuals who abused the little child who grew up to be an abusive adult, releasing them to the universe so they will be detached from your soul for future generations.

This is clearly a key component to releasing generational trauma for future generations.

It may take several attempts depending on how deep the trauma lies within you. Be patient with yourself: this is a lot, and can be quite difficult to do, but it must happen. Bless and release the souls of others to detach them from you. If you are truly able to release them, you will achieve such a sense of relief and then continue to move along on your path to the light. Your burdens will be lifted, and you will feel such an overwhelming sense of peace and calm come over your body and soul; life will become so much more peaceful and serene. You will begin to see all that is in our beautiful world.

You will be able to deal with so many situations with a sense of inner peace. You will not have the stress and dis-ease that you had before. You will approach life with a different perspective. Things will not upset or stress you the way they did before. There will be no fear, no guilt, no anger as you once had: that is all part of the past. You will now understand that there is nothing that you cannot get through. You must just leave fear in the past. Look fear square in the face and move through it; this is how it is supposed to be.

Fearlessly walk through with the confidence of our creator. Know He is by your side, know without a doubt that you will get there by walking through your fear, moving through with your new power. There is nothing more powerful than taking back your power – the power that has been there all along. Taking all of it head on and burying your burdens, When this is complete then you can live again – free from your past burdens, free from those who have hurt you, free from all that was. Freedom from it all, so that you can be all that you can be.

You must continue this process with each and every trauma that happened and go through it – to pass through to the other side.

Walking through each and every memory that was carefully placed in your locked box will present its own challenges. You will slowly accept your truth of what was, knowing that it was not your fault – not your guilt or anger to hold on to. You will let go of all those negative feelings about all that was, one at a time. You may feel all those feelings surface at different times along the way, but you must accept and release all of it until that box is empty.

All of that will be behind you. Your burdens will lighten little by little, until you no longer carry the weight of the past. You will begin your journey of creation of all that can be. All that you can create is new – NO MORE RE-CREATION of the past, as it no longer matters. Moving to creation of all that can be will be your soul's new focus going forward. Now you may begin a soul's journey of creation. What will it be?

GOD ENCOURAGES ALL TO BE PATIENT AND KIND

No one really knows what has happened in someone else's life. Humans need to be more patient and kind toward one another. If you would all treat each other with kindness and understanding, the world would heal so much quicker.

The awakening will see tremendous understanding from all vantage points. You have seen through the small examples in this writing that two souls who have gone through very similar experiences approached life so differently and created two different experiences for their children. One approached life being bitter and cruel to all he felt superior to or able to control. The other made great efforts not to be bitter or cruel and to create a loving, caring environment – but her spouse approached life from a sense of entitlement, inflicting cruelty and pain on their children. This created yet another generation of abused, angry souls – and so it continues until someone breaks the pattern of abuse for future generations.

We must shift our world away from abuse and move to a caring, nurturing, loving environment for all souls. There can no longer be this complacent attitude of continued acceptance of 'that's the way it is.'

We must awaken each and every soul to their truths and move beyond the hatred and control of all that is exists. We must allow the divine to lead us into the evolution that will heal our world.

The time for the great awakening is now. The time to move each and every human forward and bring humanity to its true purpose, the true meaning of life itself, is now! The movement must take place, the shift is already in motion; there is no stopping the power of the Divine Love to conquer all that is.

Will you take up your soul's true desire and work toward true freedom and love for all humankind?

Will you begin your journey toward truth? Will you step onto the path that has been given to you, and to each and every one of us?

Will you support all those around you, who also must take the journey to the creator – toward Divine Love and unity throughout our universe?

Make your life a journey toward the Divine. Start your journey, create the transformation, that is necessary in your life to save your soul and break the cycle of hatred and cruelty that has entrenched the world in a never-ending cycle of destruction.

GOD is calling each and every soul to him. There is only one way – that is, to follow the path – continue along the path. Move through each and every experience, feel the feelings that you must eventually let go of, and release the fear and anger of what was! Then, and only then, will you be able to leave it all behind and move forward. Continue until the box is empty. Get rid of the generational trauma that has permeated your being and tarnished your true self into denial and fear. It will all crumble before your eyes as the true strength of your soul begins to shine through. You will become stronger along the way.

Do not stop the journey; do not step off of the path. You will have the strength to complete your journey – that is how it is supposed to be – you will always have more than you need. You are never alone, and GOD's love will bring you through all that needs to happen for you to be healed.

There must be no doubt, no fear as, GOD is always here with you and with all souls.

You must believe with all of your being and then there is nothing that cannot be accomplished, nothing that you can't walk through.

Keep your faith; believe without doubt, without fear and all of it, yes all of it is for you. The world is going to heal – one soul at a time!

Remember the great awakening is here. There is no doubt, just truth for all to see.

No more lies; no more covering up the truth; all will see.

All who take the journey, all who walk the path and follow through, will have peace, freedom, Divine Love, and unity such as mankind has never seen before.

The time is now, and you must take your journey!

AGAIN WE CONTINUE
ALONG THE PATH

We continue along the path of the frightened little girl. She is now in high school, and her father does not want her to get involved in sports. That would make her muscles get bulky, and she would get fat. She gets involved anyway. She is just tired of his total control over her. She must try to get away. He is not around much, and she stays out of his way. All he does is yell, anyway. Do the chores, clean the house, help your mother, stay out of the way, and get good grades in school. Just do not tell him anything about what you are doing or thinking, and maybe you will make it through.

I could not date; I was not allowed. I went to school or to a school game, I had to come straight home. I could not go get pizza with friends on the way home, because that would require me to walk downtown. I would have to stand in line to wait to pick up food and if I were seen on the streets, I would be labeled as a bad girl – a street tramp. We could not have that. Well, one day after a basketball game, I thought no one would know. My friends were going to get a pizza, and I was in their car. I was terrified that I would get in trouble, but everyone convinced me that no one would know; we would just grab the pizza and be on our way.

Of course, we all know how that worked out. My Dad went through town after the game and just happened to pass by as we were getting out to get the pizza. Here we go again: I was a terrible person, and people would think I was a tramp. I was grounded for a month and could not go anywhere or do anything. It did not seem to matter what any of us kids did. It was always wrong, and we were always getting punished. One thing I could never figure out: as we got older the physical beatings stopped, but the verbal warfare increased. I never thought about it, as there was never time to decipher it. No time to contemplate what was happening.

We were all in survival mode, so I did not have a real opinion or original thought.

Discussing our Dad with one of my brothers, he said "We got in a confrontation and he was hitting me, so I went behind him and grabbed him, held his arms down by his sides and squeezed him so hard until he could not breathe – then Dad agreed to never beat me again, and he never did." My brother remembers being about 15 or 16 years old at the time. The physical abuse seemed to come to a truce as my brothers got older and began to stand up to him.

Control through mental abuse then became the norm. That cruelty exists, even today, as the family has progressed into their 60s and 70s. That hierarchy of power, and struggle to control all that is. Our father is incapable of giving any form of approval to any of his children; that would mean a loss of control. He still tries to stir up some controversy between the siblings by saying things that just are not true. The stories he makes up to suit his goal of dividing us never ceases to amaze each of us. It is quite a dynamic, especially to those of us still trying to believe he is someone who he is not. I think there is still one sibling who believes his antics.

The prevailing cruelty is now so evident, and has continued throughout all our lives. One day when I was struggling with my Dad and the way he treated me after my mother passed, I remember one sibling saying to me, "Dad was just so angry she died first and left him here by himself." My sibling said "I don't know why you are getting so upset, Dad has been like this all his life, he is just more so now that he is older."

The verbal abuse escalated when we were teens. He would say GOD would punish us, we would all go to Hell, we were grounded continuously, and I could never get good enough grades. Standards were different for each of us: as long as my sister passed, she was fine, but I had to make honors. Nothing less than honors was acceptable for me. I stayed up until 3 a.m. studying and memorizing my schoolwork under the covers with a small light, so I would not keep my sister awake. I was not allowed to work outside the house during high school because my father wanted those grades; my siblings were all working after school, but I was not allowed. My mother finally convinced my Dad to allow me to try out for cheerleading and when I made the team, I think he was surprised but certainly not happy. Many days I would have to walk home from practice or hitch a ride with a friend. Same rules: come straight home after the practice or a game. Again, I tried to go with friends for a pizza and got caught and grounded.

I guess I was just getting stubborn, as I continued to do the one thing that made him angry. There was just nothing acceptable about having fun or hanging out with friends; he always tried to keep me isolated.

I was 16 and finally allowed to go to a few school dances with friends. I met a guy who drove a cool car and seemed to have money in his pocket. He was friends with one of my brothers, but was really quiet. He came from a very different family than mine.

I actually felt sorry for him; his family was really messed up, I thought, even at such a young age. His father was an awful, cruel, demeaning person, physically and mentally abusive to his wife and children, an uncontrollable alcoholic, and a bully. His grandparents were unique: his grandfather was an abusive cruel man to his sweet grandmother. He beat her, cheated on her in his own home, sailed under the law with so many things that I did not understand at the time. His uncles were equally abusive, scary individuals who all treated their wives as slaves and abused them, from what I could see.

But did he really come from something different than I did? Was I brought to his world, or he to mine? Did I attract exactly what I was running from? I could not see any of it then. I just did not want to stay in my home, where I knew I was treated with total disregard. Where I had no concept of self-worth. I felt like I was cast aside and had nothing about my life that was happy or good. I never fit in. I never felt loved. I just existed. Just surviving one day at a time. There had to be more to this life, more in this world. Maybe, just maybe, if I could escape, I could figure out what that was.

ABUSE AT ALL AGES AND STAGES

As time progresses, you – and everyone around you – gets older. You might think the abuse would wane, and things would move along without all the controversy. However today, even into his mid-90s, he is still trying to manipulate and control anyone who will listen. It did not matter as kids or adults. What we did was always wrong. It did not matter how old we were, or if we had our own families and children. We could never do enough, never be enough. To this day, he secludes one child at a time and makes up the most unbelievable stories about them doing some-thing that 'hurt' him, then tries to turn everyone else in the fam-ily against them. He will take each person separately and prey on their emotions to make them think he is telling the truth. He cre-ates so much drama, calling out each and every one of us for not listening and walking away.

There are times when you just cannot listen to the stories he tells. They are completely untrue, and he forgets what he tells different people at different times. So often, we catch him in his deceitful lies. As an adult, you can look at his behavior differ-ently. You can call it out for what it is. Our mother always told us not to allow our father to do what his mother did to his family. She got them to turn on one another with her lies, and they all ended up hating each other. My mother was so afraid he would do the same to our family. He certainly has given it his best ef-fort. Some of us get it, but some do not. So goes the destruction of yet another generation of souls.

The abuse morphs and changes form over the years – but it is all abuse, whichever way you look at it. It can sometimes take a lifetime for us to recognize it, but it is all abuse plain and simple. It is hiding in plain sight. Many do not see it as a slow indoctrination of bad behavior. That behavior comes from those that are supposed to love and care for you. This pattern can be hard to decipher – but eventually that, too, is exposed.

As children we lack the collective wisdom that comes from experience. We have not yet been taught to evaluate situations as good or bad, and can't effectively draw conclusions. We are not able to clearly determine or label what the abuse actually is. As the indoctrination continues and the negative reinforcement continues, you develop distorted thoughts about these people who care for you. You are unable to form loving bonds with people who continue to damage and hurt you. We must look at that love/hate relationship that is talked about so often; the fine line between the two emotions is what you are taught, and this begins at a very young age. It develops into a distorted sense of reality that envelops you. You have never been taught what real unconditional love is.

The narcissistic parent is extremely dangerous to not only himself, his family, and friends – but also to the world. Exposing young souls to this love/hate contrast and entrapment cycle forms the basis of what they believe and will eventually act out in their lives. This allows the cycle to continue from generation to generation.

As each generation passes to the next, our souls carry the pain, resentment, hatred and trauma deep within us. When a soul begins their journey there is much to discover and process. You may think that you will discover what happened to you in this lifetime – and you might. However, this is not true for all souls.

Now you may see that the bigger discoveries are those of past generations. What was the real Truth about your parents and grandparents? Is it really what you fantasized in your mind with the limited beliefs you were given?

Is there a deeper story? Might there be a completely different version of what truly happened? Is your life truly what you thought it was? We see that children do not have the emotional maturity to discern what is happening to them in the moment as little ones. The previous generation did not have the skillset to allow them to process their experiences, either.

Your soul's journey to the truth can be very difficult. The realization that you may have to look back several generations to comprehend the truth about yourself and those who came before you may not set in for a while. However, this may be a necessary step for many souls to begin to advance on their path.

LOOKING THROUGH, NOT ATTACHING TO

As we looked at that child who was abused in every way possible, and dive into that child's lineage through her parents and grandparents, it becomes possible to see why all these things happened to her, her mother, and her grandmother. The stories, and the truth of what was and now is, all begin to come together. As much as all these women loved their children, they were unable to claim their own lives and souls. There were many others who had immense influence over their lives and the formation of their reality.

Women have been oppressed for many generations. One must wonder how this occurred. Why were men led to believe they were superior, that they needed to control their wives and children? Why did men believe they had a right to abuse their families and lord over their partners and wives like they were property and indentured servants? Why this great need to be the aggressor, to be more powerful and inflict pain and suffering to keep control and power?

How many generations must we go back to find kind, loving human beings? How far back do we need to go to find loving nurturing parents who truly taught their children about GOD's divine love and caring for others and themselves?

Free will for mankind was never meant to bestow unprecedented superiority on anyone. It was meant to allow men and women to complement each other's attributes and to have a cohesive coexistence. It was so they might share in each other's pleasures and bring forth the best in one another. If all worked together for the advancement of mankind the world would have progressed so much faster.

The evolution of mankind is so far behind all others in the universe are amazed that earth has just not progressed way beyond where you are. Many question whether mankind can get out of their own way in order for the evolution to take place.

There must be a dramatic shift in thinking. All the abuse is knocking at your doors. It is in the light for all to see. It cannot be ignored any longer. The shift must, and will, proceed with or without your consent.

Children must no longer bear the guilt, hatred, abuse and fear of the previous generations. They must be treated with compassion and true divine love by their parents. No more abuse! It must end!

Society as we know it has failed our people. Our churches have failed their people, our world leaders have failed their people, and our leaders and teachers in all walks of life have failed our children.

There must be a shift towards consciousness, a shift towards the real truth – not the made-up untruths we have told ourselves for many generations. The act of going out in public and putting on a show for others is over. The idea of 'One big happy family behind the white picket fence' is a falsehood. In truth, the white picket fence was hiding total chaos, misery, physical, mental, and sexual abuse beyond your wildest dreams.

This is not the story of one family; it is a story of everyone's family, all over the world.

Children who bear the burdens of past generations continue the abuse. Children who should be nurtured by adults are assaulted and brutalized by those who are entrusted to protect them and teach them how to love and care for the next generation.

Instead, our children have been taught all the wrong things. Everyone expects them to find their way through and be wonderful human beings. What examples of this have they seen? Children will act and react as they are taught and observe from adults.

How can previous generations expect anything different from their children, when they themselves cannot even come close to measuring up to that expectation?

When true generations of GOD's children finally stand tall and walk the path of Divine Love – when they truly cherish their relationships with their partners and children and others – then, and only then, can the world begin to heal.

Each soul is a gift to humanity, and each soul will atone at some point for what has happened. Teach your children well. Teach them to love and care for others. Teach them true compassion, caring, giving and love.

This will be the only way to save mankind. This will be the only way to repair all the damage that has been done to all souls. Begin NOW!

Take the journey. Reveal your truth and accept what was – all of it! Move forward with compassion, let the hurt go, and bring your soul back in alignment with GOD's purpose.

Stop the wheels of generational trauma dead in its tracks. Move to unite your soul with GOD. Teach your children to know GOD; to love and care for themselves and others. It must happen.

Let Go, Let GOD!

TALKING TO PAST GENERATIONS TAKES TIME

I have been on my path for some time. It has not been easy, nor will I try to tell you that your path will be easy, but there is help – and you will be given what you need to move along your path to the truth.

Although I never understood how much she really went through, I always had a special relationship with my mother. As a child, it was very difficult to see what was happening in a world of adults that seemed so secretive. My mother would never speak about what her real relationship with my dad was about. It was not until my oldest son passed away that I learned how to connect with my mother, who had passed several years prior. I knew she was there holding my son's hand as he moved beyond this Earth. There are just those profound times in your life that there is no comfort, and all you want is your Mom. I was devastated beyond my ability to comprehend this tragic loss, and had no way of reconciling it.

I first began speaking to my Mom through an intermediary. I just did not know how to communicate with her. It took some time working with a few different guides to understand that all souls have the ability to communicate with other souls, whether they are here or in the next dimension. Each of us, if we learn to quiet our minds and bodies, can eventually communicate with those who are no longer here on Earth – and, yes, with GOD as well.

MY CONVERSATIONS WITH MOM

Interestingly enough, I am usually lying in bed sleeping or trying to relax by doing my meditative breathing when I begin to have most of my communications. One night at 11:58 pm, I was awakened for what seemed to be no reason. It just seemed very quiet, and I turned on my left side and began having bubbles come up my throat. Just bubbles slowly coming up my chest and then I had a feeling someone was there.

"Mom, are you there?" I asked. A sense of calm came over me. I gently asked, "Why did you marry Dad? Did you really feel you were getting too old to marry? You were so pretty and so talented." I continued, "Why would you marry a truck driver?"

Well, she said, "he was handsome – there were very few men my age that were not already married. My dad thought it was time for me to find a husband. My dad was very definite and deliberate; he was a very ridged man. He thought a young woman should be married. I needed to find a husband – and since my sister was not married, he could not have two daughters who were not married. So, I felt like I needed to marry. I was not getting any younger."

"Mom, did you really feel trapped with dad?"

"He was nice when we dated, but he was a drunk just like his brothers. He thought he could contain his drinking, but he could not. He was terrifying after we got married. Meme always bragged about your dad, how much money he made. She was always pitting her boys against each other. I never understood, why everything was always a competition, I could never understand why. It gave your dad such a big ego. He thought he was always better than his brothers. Dad did unconceivable things and tried to make believe he was better than all his siblings. He was always having something to say about me to his mother."

"Mom, is [she] really Dad's daughter?"

"Yes, yes, she is. The other woman and I had to come up with a story that everyone would believe. It was the only way for all of us –

I had to use that to stop your Dad from drinking. He was so cruel to all you children. He was an angry drunk! He lashed out at all of us. The only way to make it stop was to threaten to expose him – so he stopped drinking as much.

He hid it well. He still drank, just not as much. It was a little more controlled – or he just waited until you kids were all in bed. I used to pretend I was sleeping many nights when he came home; that way he would just go to bed.

I knew he was out carousing but there really was not much to do about that. I was so scared that I was always afraid of everything, afraid of the dark – afraid when he was going to come home – afraid he would send me away"

"Mom when he cracked your ribs that was not from him hugging you was it?"

"No, he was angry with me."

"For what, why was he angry?"

"He did not want me to talk to the neighbor. He did not like me visiting with her. He knew we were supporting each other. He did not want me to talk to her. He was so worried that someone would find out – he was paranoid about that – so he just wanted me to know he could hurt me if I did not do what he wanted me to – there was no one for me to turn to – I was like you, feeling very alone. I wish things were different for you – I did the best I could.

I could not protect anyone from him. I could barely keep myself from him. Eventually I was able to threaten him with exposing him, and he knew I meant it.

He was very busy doing his thing in the big city for quite a while, so he was not home much until he worked locally for a trucking company not far from home.

I tried to appease him and keep him away from you as much as I could, there were just times when he made things impossible."

"What happened when my youngest brother was born?"

"It was a couple years before the neighbor's little girl of his was born.

Everyone believed the story about her and her husband, how he forced himself on her."

"But that was not true, was it?"

"No, it was not true. Dad and she had a thing and she got pregnant. I am sure Dad was drunk and kind of forced himself on her, she was ashamed and ended it abruptly with your Dad, but it was too late – the child is Dad's as far as I know. We just thought it was best for all to let sleeping dogs lie. It would have caused so much pain to tell the truth; her husband knew it was Dad. He blamed her for the indiscretion, but it was not her; your father was forceful, and it made him crazy to have me talking to her.

She told him to stay away. There was a reason for truces."

"Does her oldest daughter know?"

"Yes, she told her not to ever tell anyone."

"Somehow, I think she would tell me the truth?"

"I believe she feels your sister is too volatile and could not keep it to herself, so she did not want to tell her. She stuck with the story about her father forcing himself on her. Yes, she knows, but she might not be able to say it. She's not a young woman anymore.

Sometimes best to let sleeping dogs lie."

"What was the real reason we could not have friends to our house...Dad?"

"I could not be responsible for other children being around your father. So I needed to do something to keep them away from him; his cruelty knew no boundaries. He could not be trusted around kids."

"What about his brother?"

"He was not well when he came home from the service. He had a nervous breakdown – that was true. He was around a little bit. He was with Meme until your father had to take over for him."

"What did Dad do to me – did he use some type of probe or tool on me? What did he do to me and to my sister?"

"You were around 3 years old. Dad was in the room with you, he was angry, and he had your clothes off when he pushed your sister aside. He was fondling himself in front of you girls. I caught him hurting you."

"How, what did he do?"

"He was playing with himself and you. He had his hands all over you; he was violating you with his fingers as he pleasured himself. I gasped and he did not know what to do." "What are you doing?" I screamed – and ran out of the room – "I did not know what to do. He did not expect me to walk in. He came after me to try to cover up what he was doing. There was no undoing what I saw. I know he did it to both of you.

I just knew it...

How could we live with this? How- could- we- live- with- this! There was nothing in the world that was worse than that! What could I do – I did not protect you girls from the one person who could have hurt you like this – OH MY GOD – Now what – what do I do with this? I went to the priest. It was so difficult. He told me I had to stay; I had to work this out with my husband. I begged him to help me – he said I must go back home. GOD will show you how to forgive him.

I never wanted you girls to be hurt – I wanted to make it all go away, make it stop. Get away from him – how do we move forward? How do I stay with him?

"I see why I blocked this out. My life story is just some fantasy movie playing in my head. I made up this fairytale that you had such a wonderful marriage. I just had to block it out to make it through."

And then silence in my mind. She stopped talking. Silence was all around me.

I knew this was hard for her to tell me. This was a lot to hear all at once. It completely crushed my little story that I had created in place of the truth of my childhood. That locked box had a lot more baggage than I ever imagined. What a lot to process. It would take some time to process all this information.

THE HEALING PROCESS COMES FROM WITHIN!

Once you have cleared the old memories from your soul it will be time to heal all that has kept you from perfect health and happiness and Divine Love.

A soul needs to advance in harmony with our creator. In order to unite your soul and connect with GOD, you must look deep inside. Your soul already knows all it needs to do to bring itself in alignment with our source energy and GOD.

When we are born into this world, there are so many outside influences in our lives that we are not directed to grow in unison with our real purpose. Parents, families, friends, communities and world leaders impose so many thoughts, ideas, rules and laws that are not harmonious with our souls' innate understanding of what was, before we were born.

So many of us are drawn away from our intended purpose by all that is constantly thrust upon us, that it can take decades to bring our souls back in alignment and clear all the misdirected influences of the earthly world from our inner consciousness. All must allow themselves to understand their truth and move to the next great creation of all that can be – and make it all that is to be.

Awaken your soul to the core purpose, that is to enjoy life, live in truth and happiness, and accept the Divine Love in your deepest thoughts, words and actions. These are the center of what your soul yearns for. Deep down inside, you already have an awareness that life is supposed to be a wonderful expansive, collective experience that will move you closer to becoming one with your creator. It is what all souls wish to achieve: Unity with GOD.

When we are in this world surrounded by chaos and confusion, the struggle for power and control becomes a reality. We are aware on a deeper level that this is not what should be. We sometimes feel that we have no control over our surroundings or what is happening in the world; however, each soul must concentrate on their journey as the great awakening is occurring. It may seem that it is taking forever for our world to evolve, and on a human timescale that may be true. It has taken centuries to get to where we are today. Man's desire for power and control continues to hinder the progress of this world.

Know that the awakening is now happening at warp speed. It has begun with hundreds and thousands of souls who are now taking their journeys. Now your soul must begin its journey. It has started with you reading this book.

You must take the first step onto the path and begin your journey now. Go through the process of healing your past. Move to the present which will begin your soul's process of creation.

The re-creation of what was, and the acceptance of truth, has moved many souls past what was and onto the pathway to creation.

Let's go and create all that your imagination can conceive – and so much more.

THE CONVERSATIONS WITH MY GRANDMOTHER

Back two generations and connecting with my maternal Grand-mother.

It was very quiet; I was awakened again in the late-night hours. I asked, *"Is this grandma?"*

"Yes. It is me. You have been asking to speak with me, so I have come to talk to you."

The first question I asked: how did she meet my grandfather?

"My dad left when I was too little to remember. My mother worked at the mill. One day she met a gentleman who was an engineer who went from mill to mill in eastern Connecticut checking on the production. He had a conversation with my mother, and he was looking for a sweet young girl to marry. My mother brought him home to meet me. I was out of 8th grade, but too young to work. Mom thought he was well off and would make a good husband. He would take care of me. He was well dressed and a nice-looking man. There were not many options for a young girl in those days, in the early 1900s. My mother wanted me to marry and be taken care of. It was very important to her to have me taken care of.

I was younger than him by 10 years. We were not able to see each other alone. We had to have a chaperone. He decided he wanted to marry me."

I asked, "How old were you?"

"I was about 18 when we married. He was a very difficult man and definitely made all the decisions. I was a housewife and he wanted children.

Women got married, stayed home and had children. I would teach the girls to sew and clean house, do laundry and cook. I was the homemaker, and he would provide for us. I would think sometimes, I wished I could have been more, do more but your grandfather would not have it. I was his wife and that was it. "Fait accompli" and there was to be no discussion about it.

Your Aunt left on a sour note and never returned. I blamed your grandfather for that. He did not have to crush her heart – but he was just so stubborn. It was always his way or no way. I lost my oldest daughter. She was bitter all her life and died bitter. Your poor mother lost her only sister. I think that is why she wanted four children, so you would always have someone who was family in your lives. She did not want you to be like her with a sister who did not care about her. It was not your mother's fault. Her sister was just mad at the world, poor child."

"Did you love Grandpa?"

"It was sort of an arranged marriage. I was to marry him, take care of his house, be his wife, have children and he would take care of us. He was disappointed that we did not have a boy. I did not want any more children, so it was what it was.

Women were supposed to obey their husbands. Not sure who came up with that, this was what my mother told me, "Just do what he says and hopefully he will stay with you – not like your dad who left me." Be careful, do not make him angry, and look the other way when he has his indiscretions and maybe he will stay. With that as my belief, you can see why I did not want any more children. I did not want to have to raise them alone like my mother did.

I never really knew my Dad. He left when I was very young. I did not want that for my children. I know that you understand that. We love our children. We want what is best. Your mom was getting older out of high school and working at the mill. It did not look like she would marry; your grandfather was very worried that she would be a spinster. When she met your dad, he seemed ambitious; he thought he might have a son if she married him.

Grandpa did not see that he was very young, and very angry at the world – just like your Mom's sister. He felt that everyone did everything to him and he was going to show the world. I was concerned but your grandfather made the decision again, I had nothing to say about the matter.

I prayed for your mother, I prayed that her husband would treat her right – but that never happened. He was overbearing, cruel and got involved with bad people. Grandpa knew some of those men from work and he encouraged your Dad – because he could make good money, but he sold his soul for money and my sweet daughter paid the price.

I could not help your mother. She had child after child. Your grandfather became ill and passed. Then I became ill shortly after. I wanted so much for your aunt to come here and help your Mom get away. But your mother hid her pain; she refused to talk about it. He was just like her father, headstrong, always right, roving eye, and drank too much.

She already had three children and a fourth on the way when I left the Earth – I tried to help her from here. She was so alone, and your father hid his cruelty from her aunts and uncles. They thought he was a good guy, and your mother never told them the truth. What he was involved with or how he abused her was never anything she could discuss.

Your father isolated her, so she had no one, no friends, and the one she did have – ended up having an affair with your Dad, and a baby. That man, it just never ended. Then for your Mom to have to watch that child – she knew was his – grow up right next door. She had to have an alliance with her to keep your dad in line. I saw what happened to her children at the hands of her husband – cruelty and abuse beyond imagination. He was a cruel, angry, hateful person. If only I could have changed things, helped her get away – I loved your Mom – she was so special to me, but I could not protect her from your Dad. Your grandfather thought he was great, just wanted someone to take your mother and take care of her. He never thought of how he would abuse her.

And then to see what he did to the children, you were all just babies, and he abused you and did not give a damn about it – like it was his right to physically, sexually and mentally abuse each and every one of you. It just makes me sick.

It made your mother sick, but she did not know who to turn to – when she finally got the courage to go to the priest for help, he just sent her home. What useless, weak men, men of the church, men of the cloth – just despicable drunks. They could not even live with themselves for what they did. They knew it was wrong not to save the women and children from the abuse, but they did nothing.

Their complacency ruined generations of children. Those they abused and those they allowed to be abused under their watch, cover it up, cover it up; GOD saw it all!

Yes, I saw how this life was hard, for me even when I was so young, I did not want any more children, and I made sure no more children were born after your mother – I made sure.

He pushed your mother into her marriage – he was so afraid that she would not have anyone to take care of her; she was old by the standards back then."

I asked, "Did Grandpa know what my dad was doing when he went to the city? "

"Yes, he knew, and he was involved as well. It was a dangerous time, the war, the mafia – the murders – the power culture. Your mother and I were frightened to death; it was a scary time for women. It was nothing for them to come and kill your children – rape your wife – beat your boys, maim or kill them.

It was very real, and your father was in the thick of it, traveling around and then coming back here. I prayed for your Mom and you children, and the perpetrator was your own father – such an angry fellow. Always in competition with his brothers, your father, tried to win the favor of your grandmother; she was a mean old woman. Another one who was angry with the world, her husband abused her, and she would never let that happen again. She would never remarry even if her children would starve to death. She sent them all away for quite some time until her brother brought them here. She was always angry like your father and his brothers, all a bunch of bullies and drunks – and this is what your grandfather gave my poor sweet girl to – a life of misery and abuse. And my poor grandchildren: a life of abuse at the hands of their father.

Your dad could have chosen to be a good husband and a good father. He could have chosen to be kind and loving. He chose not to be. Then he intimidated your mother into hiding his hatred for all of you with his threats and abuse.

He will have to atone for what he has done. Do not feel bad for not seeing him; he is miserable. He knows your mother has given you the truth and he cannot live with himself, and GOD has decided to let him sit with all of it.

He is too damn proud to ask for forgiveness or even admit what he did.

That's on him. I was proud of you for taking the steps you needed to help yourself and your children and grandchildren. It is not an easy road, but you have come through it.

Your sister still needs help, but she still denies the Truth. Hopefully she will get it. Your brother knows what he did to you girls and your brothers; he will not acknowledge it, but he is uncomfortable around you now as well.

Yes, write the book, change the names if need be – but write the book – publish the book – I am fine with it. Your mom will be, too.

It takes enormous courage to do what you are doing. Do not worry about others' opinions; it does not matter. Your two younger brothers will not care. Your sister will get antsy about it, but will have to accept it. You and your daughter will be teaching others to face and accept their past, their pain, and show others the path to healing their souls. It is supposed to be how you help people – and you will.

I had to wait until you were ready for me. I love you and I watch over you - always."

"Grandma, I wish I could have met you. I so wanted someone to love me as a child."

"I did love you, just from here. I saw what they did to you, and it gave me great pain. I was watching over you. Your poor mother was just trying to survive. I watch over your sister as well. She was an angry parent, especially to her son, but was not very nice to her daughter either. They knew it as well. They were grateful for you being around to smooth her down. She was just abused like you, and never got over it. She could have chosen to be happy, but she chose to be bitter. She knows it now but could not see it then. She will come around eventually. Mom and I will talk to her some more.

There is another girl who is your other sister. You know it, and so does she, but she will not admit it yet.

We will gently tell her the truth; let's see if she listens.

Keep writing and include it all, and do not worry. Remember, you're doing this to help others. It is not really about you. It is a story that will resonate with many far and wide. It is for healing; it is what needs to be told. You are a messenger, and you have quite a message."

And then there was just quiet, in the darkness, just silence.

THE LITTLE GIRL NEEDS TO HEAL!

The little girl who hid the box of awful things, that awful Truth, so no one was able to find it, so she would not have to face or process the truth of the past.

Well, once she did begin to look at it – once she did face the truth and began the journey – it became more and more apparent to her that it was not her fault. She did not create all that was. She did not have to accept the blame, the guilt and all that fear. The anguish was real, but she did not cause that which had tarnished her soul and damaged her life. She was not the one at fault for this – not at fault for any of this.

One tragic incident at a time was inflicted upon her, thrust upon that innocent child who was defenseless to cope and carry all of the shame and guilt that was imposed upon her. We must now evaluate these horrific violations that passed through her soul, crossing her path to the Light. We must see those things that had kept her from GOD.

The yearning of your soul has brought her and you to where we are now. Even through all of it, this tiny child knew deep inside that this was not the way it should be – but was not capable of recognizing what it *should* be. Only the advancement and progression of the human experience could give the clarity necessary to discern what had to be. Only the progression of a soul's journey could light up the path to the true meaning of it all. As the years passed, many more transgressions would have to take place before this damaged little soul would have the ability to see what had been done to her.

There were so many more years of damage to come. The journey into the deep, dark world of the abused can go on for many years, as in this case. It often can take many decades before we are able to see that we do not have to continue on this path.

Until one feels that they are worthy of happiness and love, the darkness will continue. This is a very important statement for anyone who has been abused in this human world. Your ability to feel loved, and your capacity to love, are gravely diminished by those perpetrators; they seem to have taken it all. There are many twists and turns on this bumpy road.

Many times, when the feeling of being helpless and alone overwhelms the human mind, you may feel like there is no hope – just despair. As you progress through the path on your journey these feelings will begin to fall from your being, and as you walk through the past trauma it will be shed from your heart and soul. It will be behind you as you continue your journey. Eventually you will see you are capable of being bigger and stronger than all that was.

Sometimes you may feel so empty your despair may feel like it is taking over – but this too shall pass. Just continue to walk one step at a time and remember that patience is a virtue. I know I've said it before, but it needs to be repeated. There seemed to be no one on the path to help guide this little girl to safety. She always had her faith and talked to GOD many times, but she felt the need to cover up what was happening and not ask GOD for what she really needed. The shame she felt caused her to hide from all that was. All the guilt and shame were misplaced and she could not find a way to express it, even to GOD, as she was taught to hide it all. Keep it to herself never tell anyone what happened in that home.

There was nowhere for her to turn, and so it continued even into adulthood. She never developed the skillset to recognize the abuse. She was never able to understand that this was not meant to be. It just was, and she lived the warped truth she had come to know for many years.

The hatred and abuse continued throughout her life; there were many more years of abuse. The names of the perpetrators changed, but the story of abusive people in her life continued. When her family saw what was happening to her, they all chose to be complacent – just like the priest her mother had begged for help so many years before. Was it really choosing not to deal with it? After all, they were taught the same cruel behaviors. Could it be that maybe they were all going through their own journey? Maybe they were still in survival mode, in their own worlds. When you are damaged, it is hard to look beyond your damaged world and lend your hand to help another.

As you peel away the hurt and pain and those tiny bubbles continue to surface, you gain a new perspective on all that was. As the evolution of your soul progresses – and it will, at its own pace – you will begin to see the light peeking through, one small ray at a time. It cannot be stopped once you are on the path, unless you choose to stop it. Continue no matter how difficult it seems; always continue to move along the path.

The healing began on this journey. At first, she did not recognize what was happening. She was in so much pain from losing her son that everything was overshadowed by her grief. She felt so alone, everyone was living in fear. It was during the pandemic; our churches failed their people, so there were no services and no support for the people in our communities. When everyone needed their community's support the most, all leaders cowered in fear.

She would begin the process alone, with just her husband and two children. Thank God for them. When the realization came that she was just spiraling deeper and deeper into the dark abyss, this was the time at which the awakening and the journey began for her. There were signs from above from many who loved her who had gone to the other side. They came from all directions; some from guides here on Earth, and some from guides above. It took some time to recognize these signs. She read a lot of books, one after another. She could not seem to read fast enough. Her soul knew it was time, time for exactly what she did not know – but it was definitely time to heal and move forward to what is meant to be.

As she began to process that grief of losing her son, all the other memories began to surface. Questions started to come: what really happened as a child? The things that were in that box began to surface, and the bubbles started to burst one at a time. It seemed like there was nothing that could compare with that state of being after losing her son. She began to feel anything and everything that surfaced. Nothing, absolutely nothing, could even come close to what she was feeling at that point in time.

Her world of secrets that were so tightly locked in the box started to appear; one at a time, and then many all at once. The practice of meditation had helped unleash all that was. It had to happen, she was already on the path, finally; after a lifetime of pain and grief and hiding the truth, it was all unfolding. The information was given in many different messages. It came through her son who had passed, in her meditations, and in her sleep. It came from guides here on Earth. It came from guides above, who would bring messages through her writing and in her sleep.

The writings had so many details of the events. It was extremely hard to deny. The ringing in her ears and the vibrations were indisputable proof of what was happening. There was no doubt that many would bring messages in all forms. The human mind cannot process sometimes. Messages come through, but they don't always come from only one source. You may get information from many sources; pay attention to what is being put in front of you. It all is part of the plan. The information will flow if you have faith and believe that GOD is working through many ways to find the best method of communication for you.

The unfolding of all that was will take time, and the effort you put into your heart and soul will be rewarded with peace and contentment like you have never felt before. All the anxiety, pain, and anger will start to dissipate into the universe.

When we no longer deny our truth, then the healing begins. You must move on from denial and accept all that was. You do not have to agree with – or like – what is being told to you. In fact, you likely will not like the truth as it is presented to you; it will be hard to digest in most cases. But as you begin – as she also began – to realize, what happened in the past must be acknowledged in order for your soul to heal. Then, it will all begin.

The relief of knowing, then the acceptance of what was, and releasing the pain, the guilt, and anger, becomes easier as each bit of information is released to your conscious mind. The healing moves faster as you realize that you should not judge. Let go of the judgment, which is not your soul's purpose. GOD will deal with those things on his own time. Your soul's journey is to move through the steps for each experience, blessing and releasing that soul to GOD in order to attain the peace, contentment and happiness you deserve; always moving toward the Divine Love of GOD.

Going back and seeing that frightened little toddler being abused by her father was extremely difficult for the girl. The pain of that reality had consumed her for some time. It seemed inconceivable to her – even now, decades later. At some level she knew it was true, even though she needed to hear it from different sources. That began the real search for the Truth of what was. She needed a greater understanding to process this information. A closer connection to the one place where there could be no denial. That place was with GOD. She prayed that she would be able to process and move through all of it. She went deeper into meditation. She chose guided meditations at first, learning the techniques to relax and then working on them over and over. The ringing in her ears became more and more prominent, for longer and longer periods of time. The writings in the middle of the night got longer and longer. She learned to ask questions – and amazingly, the answers came in her writing.

She learned that compassion is also a virtue. Looking at the movie playing in her head, it was easy to want to take care of the poor little girl being abused, take her and remove her, hug her, console her and promise to protect her going forward.

Signs continued to come to her every day, as if there was support all around her. The feeling of loneliness began to dissipate. It was like she now had all the support she needed to help the little girl and to eventually help herself. There is support if you look for it. It does not have to come from earthly sources. Sometimes it comes from the Divine. What a revelation that was for the little girl. All this, right here right in front of her.

The sense of peace begins to flow as you learn to let go!

GOD SPEAKS TO ME

All these years of trying to make believe all was well, just like your mother and grandmother did, had to come to an end. Never speaking their truth was not good for them or mankind. The atrocities had to come to light. It is past time to heal my children for the next generations.

I have put in motion many feminine souls to begin working together. They will bring my messages, and they will move my people to the next step of evolution. The energy in the universe is already gathering and swirling around, ready to infiltrate those I have chosen to lead. You are here reading this now and will see through this messenger many of these people. I can wait no longer for the evolution to take place on its own. Divine intervention is the only way to save your world, and so it shall be.

If you are called, you must listen and take your place. You must step into the light. If it is your calling, you will shine through the rest, you will be more of my messengers. There will be many; you will band together to bring peace and love to the world. Things will change and you will all be part of the change. Those who deny me will perish, as it is written.

The rulers will step aside, it will be like David and Goliath! My army of feminine energy shall sweep the world. This is where true compassion for all mankind will come from. Men have gotten too far off the path. They have reached a point of no return, and must step aside for true healing to begin. There is a lot of healing that must take place in order for you to survive.

Remember what I told you: there are more than enough resources for all to have what they need. The wars and fighting for superiority must stop!

Each of my messengers will step into the light as I call them. No hiding behind the veil; no worrying about what may happen, as I am here to guide each and every one of you. I do not falter, I do not fail. When GOD is involved, we will always, yes, always PREVAIL.

There is to be no doubt, no fear. You are to believe, and I will deliver your world to peace, love and harmony as it should be.

This is what I want for all my souls, and it must be for all to move through the evolution of time.

There must be healing for all my battered and beaten-down souls. There must be healing for all mankind.

This little girl is no longer alone; there is an overwhelming sense of peace knowing that all the messages she is receiving are real. "Her son is with her mother. They are very close. They are well. They are with me". This message comes over and over. Her mother told her all she needed to do is let the truth come forward. Her grandmother gave her some clarity as to what it was like when women were so helpless and unable to speak up, or become what they could have been. The control placed over women through intimidation and fear for their lives – and the lives of their children – was tremendous. This was passed to the mother, who had tremendous strength to keep her family together under the most extreme circumstances – then down to the little girl. It was all ruining mankind, filtering right through generations of souls.

WHERE OH WHERE DOES IT END!

Well, the healing is here, the burdens are lifting. The next generations have been tarnished by this generational trauma, but they will not stand for it; the time is now to speak up!

The young women of the current generations will speak up. They will be the examples of stopping the abuse with their children; they will recognize and eliminate abusive behavior from their children's lives. They are being taught to speak up, to use their voices, and not to hide the trauma in the locked boxes of the past. They will not stand for locking things in the box. They will not stand for being silenced by the male energy in their lives. They will show the world a better way.

Oh yes, they will; it is happening already. They will recognize all that was and know they have the power to change it. They will be our next generation of warriors.

What a wonderful world this can and will be for future generations. It is so exciting to know that they will finally be heard. They will change the world and bring it back in harmony with all that it should be. Let it all begin with life, liberty and the pursuit of happiness and freedom for all souls, everywhere!

GOD EXPLAINS THE GENERATIONS BEFORE US

Generations ago, there was no help or assistance for women and children. It did not matter where they lived throughout the world. The women were battered and beaten, as were the children, for centuries everywhere on Earth. It happened throughout the lands, on every corner of my world. This is why the problem runs so deep: it was everywhere.

The overwhelming fear of being left alone and abandoned was a central theme throughout your life. It began generations before you, with your great grandmother – when her husband left her. He was cheating on her, and she could not bear it. She did not want to live with a man who was present only when he felt like it, so she asked him to leave. He was just going to do what he wanted, no matter what. So she felt abandoned when he did finally leave. She actually thought he would stay, but that did not happen.

The fear in your grandmother was instilled in her by her mother's loss. Your grandmother lived in fear of abandonment all her life. She was silenced and full of fear, your grandmother. Your grandmother's fear resonated well beyond just abandonment. She actually feared for her life and the lives of her girls. There was no way she would have any more children, to worry herself to death about. What might happen to more poor innocent children? There was no other choice than to make sure no more children were born.

If your grandmother had any support or any way to leave and make sure her children were safe – had she seen any other options – she would have left. She had grown up in fear with her single mom, who just scraped by, and she did not know how she could get away from your grandfather and keep her children safe from him or the other people he was involved with.

Your poor mother felt the same way. After her parents had passed there was just no one to help her. All she thought about was: how would she be able to take care of all of you? She felt so trapped. (Sound familiar?)

 She felt trapped just like you did; the fear of losing your children was overwhelming, and they threatened you just like your father threatened your mother. Your Dad threatened to hurt her and her children; she was in quite a predicament, with no path to see her way clear of your Dad and his cronies. Your Mom was just trying to keep all of you out of harm's way. She was trying to keep you away from someone who was supposed to love and protect you all. The biggest threat came from your father and his partners in crime, as they say.

You know who I am referring to: the devil she was forced to sleep with was her husband. Isn't there some movie called "Sleeping with the Enemy"? That is what your mom lived with every day. The biggest threat to her and her children was living in her home. The evil came from within.

GOD EXPLAINS THE FEAR OF ABANDONMENT

For many women, fear of abandonment by someone who they have been made to fully depend upon is an extremely overpowering emotion. Over the generations, women were better able to go to work and get jobs that paid a little more. Eventually they were actually able to support themselves; this set in motion the ability for them to survive without having to depend on someone else for their basic needs. This began an evolution in your society. Women began to very quietly have choices. They no longer needed to depend solely on the mercy of someone else to eat and have a roof over their heads.

This shift brought about big changes in family structures and the ability for women to seek different lives. Unfortunately, these new structures brought about a whole new set of challenges. Now they needed to provide all the household necessities, as well as trying to provide stability to the family structure. Women still needed to provide the nurturing and love that the children needed, and emotional support for all around them. They were alone to teach the children morals, values, and faith in GOD, as well.

This new structure – for one person to provide all of everything – is quite a daunting task for anyone. To be on their own and do it all: be the provider, the housekeeper, the teacher, the nurturer, the masculine and feminine energy and perform all the roles needed in a family unit –became nearly impossible.

GOD SPEAKS ABOUT BROKEN FAMILIES

Many family units disintegrate before your eyes. Being all of everything to everyone – and fighting the battle daily against the other parent who is no longer present in the daily lives of their children – is completely exhausting.

One soul was not meant to have all these burdens alone. One soul cannot do all and be all of everything to everyone in their family.

These near-impossible expectations were placed on so many single souls who were left to fend for themselves by the death of a partner, separation, or divorce. This has created such a different set of circumstances for the one with the children. It was an impossible journey for one soul.

There was the constant taunting from the non-present parent, which is much more than most could bear. The children were divided in their loyalties to each parent; the tug-of-war, in most cases, created its own hell on Earth for the primary parent. Never mind the burdens of making sure that all children were cared for while the primary parent was working. That is an immense burden, to make sure each family member is well cared for in your absence.

The guilt was overwhelming for these parents. Trying to keep up with all the expectations of the children; not to mention all the judgement from everyone around them. Judgment was rendered by their families, friends, churches, schools, children's friends and their parents – and the community at large. Many were ostracized just for the fact that they were not what was considered a traditional family unit. All these souls were doing was trying to survive as best they could.

Now, do you really wonder why some parents chose to leave your Earth?

Many could no longer bear all of that burden.

The children were damaged from all of it; the effects are passed down to the next generation and as the children judge their parents less, less they be judged by others; It just goes on and on.

We must stop all of this. We must get all souls on their journey to healing. It is the only way to heal my world. The only way. Move my souls along the path; it must be done.

WHEN GOD SPEAKS ALL SOULS MUST TAKE HEED!

This is the final message for this book. Know that the young girl is now a woman warrior, able to communicate with past generations. I have made it so.

The awakening is happening all around you, and it will continue.

You will tell all; the time is here; the time is now.

I will summon them. Those who are listening will journey toward the truth.

You must sit and wait for this to happen; it will be soon.

A new agreement of collective souls who will praise justice and equality, and freedom for all will emerge –

We will show my people – tell them how to come back to me.

Show them how to journey back to the truth.

Yes, you have done it, and now –You must show others!

MESSAGE FROM THE AUTHOR

After many years of walking through life with blinders on, I feel like I have been led to my purpose. I will continue my journey to bring GOD's messages as received for as long as He chooses me as a messenger.

My journey has taken way too long to begin. After many years on Earth, I was led to the path out of the overwhelming grief from the loss of my oldest son. Total despair led me to the path and at that very moment, I knew there was no other way. There is only one way, one path. There was no longer any way to deny it.

You must know the journey is a lifelong journey. All souls must come to the Awakening throughout the world. Know that my journey was not unique: there have been many similar to me, and I hope this book helps the masses of GOD's wounded warriors in our world to heal and move forward on the path back to oneness, back to Divine Love, back to GOD.

All souls are being led to the Path.

All souls must choose to step on the path.

Each and every one must begin their journey.

It must happen to save our world!

Each soul must begin their "Journey to the Awakening."

If you take one message from this book, may it be that you must

Have No Doubt, No Fear, Have Faith and Believe!

God hears all your prayers; he has given you a path. Know this message is for you!

Made in United States
North Haven, CT
05 September 2023

41164944R10087